おべんとう
Obento
DELUXE > STUDENT BOOK

4th EDITION

Peter Williams
Sue Xouris
Kyoko Kusumoto

NELSON
CENGAGE Learning

Australia • Brazil • Japan • Korea • Mexico • Singapore • Spain • United Kingdom • United States

Obento Deluxe Student Book
4th Edition
Peter Williams
Sue Xouris
Kyoko Kusumoto

Publishing editor: Jana Gabriel
Editor: Carla Morris
Senior editor: Penny Analytis
Senior designer: Miranda Costa
Cover designer: Studio Pounce
Photo research: Wendy Duncan
Production controllers: Tanya Wasylewski and Jem Wolfenden
Illustrations: OK Boss, Studio Pounce, Yuko Fujita
Typesetter: Polar Design

Any URLs contained in this publication were checked for currency during the production process. Note, however, that the publisher cannot vouch for the ongoing currency of URLs.

Acknowledgements

The Publisher would like to credit and acknowledge the following sources for photographs: Contents: p. x iStockphoto, Getty Images, Shutterstock.com; p. xi Corbis/Ronnie Kaufman/Larry Hirshowitz, Corbis/Haruyoshi Yamaguchi, Alamy; p. xii Corbis/Michael S. Yamashita, Shutterstock.com; p. xiii Kiewa College, Ioan-Liviu Orletchi, Markane Sipraseuth; design images: Daruma doll, ink splashes, lucky cat, chopsticks, corkboard, rice, origami frogs, pencil, smart phone Shutterstock.com; soy sauce container, sweets, lacquered chopsticks iStockphoto; fruit drink bottles Robert Simons; Ken Hutchinson

For product information and technology assistance,
in Australia call **1300 790 853**;
in New Zealand call **0800 449 725**

For permission to use material from this text or product, please email
aust.permissions@cengage.com

National Library of Australia Cataloguing-in-Publication Data
Obento Deluxe Student Book / Peter Williams, Sue Xouris, Kyoko Kusumoto

4th ed.
9780170196826 (pbk.)

Japanese language--Textbooks for foreign speakers--English.

495.682421

Cengage Learning Australia
Level 7, 80 Dorcas Street
South Melbourne, Victoria Australia 3205

Cengage Learning New Zealand
Unit 4B Rosedale Office Park
331 Rosedale Road, Albany, North Shore 0632, NZ

For learning solutions, visit **cengage.com.au**

Printed in China by China Translation & Printing Services.
1 2 3 4 5 6 7 17 16 15 14 13

Welcome!

Welcome to *Obento Deluxe*, the first book for middle-school students in the Obento series.

This book contains 12 units that introduce a variety of interesting topics. The topics are relevant to your everyday world and range from families and pets, to hobbies and what you do in your free time. You will learn to communicate with Japanese students your own age – to talk about your home life, leisure activities, friends and school life – and to function in the Japanese-speaking world.

As with all the books in the Obento series, you are encouraged to use every aspect of language learning to communicate in Japanese. In each unit you will find sentence patterns, vocabulary and exercises that equip you to communicate in Japanese. Even so, you do not need to understand everything you hear or read – situations requiring guesswork and gestures play an important part in conversation.

In addition to the above features, the *Obento Deluxe Student Book* is supported by a Workbook, Audio Pack, Teacher's Edition, an app and the Obento website, which can be found at www.nelsonlanguages.com.au.

Together, this book and its components provide the essentials for learning Japanese and finding out about Japanese people.

この　ほんで　日本ごの　べんきょうを
たのしんで　ください。

About the series

Student Book

The Student Book is clearly laid out and well paced. It suits students of all levels and presents all the skills needed for language learning. It includes images of Japan, *manga* stories, sentence drills and activities, and plenty of opportunities for intercultural reflection and discussion.

NelsonNetBook

The *Obento Deluxe* NelsonNetBook is an ebook that can be used online or offline. It has interactive links and 'hot spots' that give you access to a variety of multimedia resources via the web. Students can add notes, weblinks and audio recordings, and teachers can use it to share their personalised version with the class.

It is available to individual students and to schools (via a site licence).

Workbook, CD & DVD

The Workbook offers a wealth of consolidating and reinforcing exercises to revise language and structures, plus:
- a CD with the audio recordings for the listening tasks
- a DVD of cultural videos as well as the unit theme videos (with and without subtitles) that exemplify the language covered.

ISBN 9780170196826

Audio Pack

The Audio CDs are recorded with native speakers and contain recordings of:

- selected texts from the Student Book (including songs!)
- listening exercises for the Workbook
- listening exercises for the unit tests and study guides.

Teacher's Edition & DVD

- A full colour wraparound version of the Student Book with handy margin notes on how to conduct the lessons; suggested pathways; extension activities; as well as references to the Worksheets, Workbook and digital resources
- DVD with unit tests, worksheets, audio transcripts and Workbook solutions
- Access to the teacher website, which includes chapter PDFs of the Student Book, access to NelsonNetBook (for adopting schools), and comprehensive unit teaching plans and curriculum grids.

Note: additional teaching material is available on the DVD with the Teacher's Edition.

Obento Website

The *Obento Deluxe* website at **www.nelsonlanguages.com.au** offers a comprehensive suite of engaging digital resources for students, and includes:

- a variety of interactive activities
- Play 'n' Say (featuring hundreds of words and phrases for listening and speaking practice)
- Kana-chan game (for *hiragana*, *katakana* and *kanji* practice)
- *Manga* Movies (animated *manga*)

… to name just a few!

Obento App (iPhone, iPod Touch and iPad)

You can download the app from iTunes. It is a great way to revise the Obento vocabulary. It is easy and fun! For more information, contact the relevant state sales representative.

ISBN 9780170196826

About this book

Obento Deluxe is divided into 12 units.

The メニュー (menu) page of each unit is a summary of what you will learn and be able to do when you have finished the unit.

いただきます

いただきます is said by Japanese people at the start of a meal, and the いただきます section is where you get started with each unit. Pick up the key language of the unit by listening to the CD, looking at the *manga* and trying to guess what the people are saying.

You will find the unit's language patterns printed in bold text. New vocabulary (in red) is explained on the おしょうゆ pages.

どんなあじ？

どんなあじ？ means 'what flavour?' Get a taste of the new language by listening to the patterns in the *manga* and practising them. Play the CD and say the new words while you look at the examples.

つくりましょう！

つくりましょう！ means 'let's make it!' Start to put things together in conversations, role-plays and puzzles – or in an email. You will find all sorts of text types that are great for practising reading, writing and speaking. Read the tips for remembering new words and building your confidence. The more you do in つくりましょう！ the easier you will find Japanese.

べんきょうのベン

Brainy Ben brings you the new *hiragana*, *katakana* and *kanji* in the べんきょうのベン section of each unit. The charts, which show both the new characters and the ones already learnt in previous units, help you to read the alphabet and mimic the pronunciation.

> Writing takes practice, practice and more practice. That is how students in Japan learn to write, and you will perfect it in the same way.

ISBN 9780170196826

ごはんとおかず

ごはんとおかず means 'rice and side dishes'.

The ごはん (rice) in a Japanese おべんとう (lunch box) provides the foundation of the meal, and the ごはん section is the language foundation of the unit. Use the sample sentences in ごはん to see how the grammar works.

To this we add おかず (side dishes) to give the grammar its flavour. The core vocabulary is colour coded and can be substituted with other words of the same colour in the unit. There is also extra vocabulary relevant to the topic.

テーブルマナー

The テーブルマナー (table manners) section gives you information about Japanese people and how they live – their customs, culture and traditions. Have a look at Japanese culture in relation to your customs and how you live.

おはし

In Japan, you pick up your food using おはし (chopsticks). In this section you will find out about the skills that will help you 'pick up' Japanese.

おかし

Take a break to sing a song, play a game or do a craft activity. Learning should include some fun and an occasional おかし (sweet).

おしょうゆ

In the same way that おしょうゆ (soya sauce) adds flavour to food, the expressions in this section will give flavour and authenticity to your Japanese. The words here will also help you to sound more natural when speaking Japanese.

せつめい

At the back of the book is the handy reference section, せつめい (explanation), in which the grammar of each unit is explained in further detail.

All the vocabulary for the Student book, Workbook and audio recordings is listed in a comprehensive glossary at the back of this book.

ISBN 9780170196826

Icons used in this book

This book contains the following icons to guide you to extra material and resources.

 This icon directs you to an audio recording that is in the Audio Pack, and is hotspotted in the NelsonNetBook.

 This icon directs you to manga movie animations on the website.

 This icon directs you to external websites in order to learn more about a topic or to complete an activity.

 This icon directs you to the Play 'n' Say on the website where you can listen to these words and phrases, record yourself saying them and play back your recording to compare.

 This icon directs you to a relevant cultural slideshow in the Teacher's Edition DVD.

 This icon directs you to a relevant video clip on the Student Workbook DVD.

 This icon directs you to the website to complete a drag-and-drop or similar interactive task.

 This icon means there are worksheets, activity sheets, puzzles or research tasks. They are located in the Teacher's Edition DVD and are hotspotted in the NelsonNetBook.

ISBN 9780170196826

Meet the Obento cast

Nakayama Gakuen is a middle school in the outer suburbs of Tokyo. This year, the school is hosting a group of international exchange students from around the world. All of the international students are being hosted by Nakayama Gakuen students and their families.

One international student, Ben, is not on exchange and has lived in Japan for some time with his family. He knows the ins and outs of school life in Japan and is doing his best to make the new arrivals feel at home.

Yuki Matsuda
Age: 14
Home town: Tokyo
まつだ　ゆき

Ben Summers
Age: 14
Home town: Perth
べん　さまーず
ベン　サマーズ

Emma Jennings
Age: 12
Home town: Auckland
えま　じぇにんぐず
エマ　ジェニングズ

Kate Henderson
Age: 12
Home town: Sydney
けいと　へんだそん
ケイト　ヘンダソン

Tony Cruise
Age: 14
Home town: Toronto
とにー　くるーず
トニー　クルーズ

Harjono Sudarga
Age: 13
Home town: Jakarta
はじょーの　すだーがー
ハジョーノ　スダーガー

Takako Moriyama
Age: 13
Home town: Tokyo
もりやま　たかこ

Yuusuke Sato
Age: 14
Home town: Tokyo
さとう　ゆうすけ

Kenichi Fukuda
Age: 14
Home town: Tokyo
ふくだ　けんいち

Mr Nakamura
Home town: Tokyo
なかむらせんせい

ISBN 9780170196826

Contents

Unit 4

かぞく
Family

All about
- Family

Culture
- Families in Japan

Language patterns
- Asking how many people are in someone's family and responding
  なん人　かぞく　ですか。
  三人　かぞくです。
- Saying who is in your family
  おとうさんと　おかあさんと　わたし　です。
- Asking someone if they have any pets and responding
  ペットが　いますか。
  はい、　いぬが　います。
  いいえ、　いません。

Text types
- Family profile

Hiragana
う、え、く、そ、ぬ、ね、ひ、へ、も、り、る、が、ぎ、じ、ぞ

Katakana
ペ

Unit 5

ワンワン、ガーガー
Woof woof, quack quack

All about
- Pets

Culture
- *Momotaro*, a Japanese folktale

Language patterns
- Asking what someone's pet is and responding
  ペットは　なん　ですか。
  ペットは　いぬ　です。
- Asking whose pet it is and describing pets
  だれの　ペット　ですか。
  けんいちくんの　ペット　です。
  ペットは　うるさい　です。
- Asking what pets eat and drink and responding
  きんぎょは　なにを　たべますか。
  きんぎょは　えさを　たべます。
  ねこは　なにを　のみますか。
  ねこは　みずを　のみます。

Text types
- Folktale
- Poster
- PowerPoint presentation

Hiragana
- ち、つ、の、ふ、む、め、や、れ、ろ、を、ず
- *Hiragana* sound changes and combination sounds

Unit 6

パスタがすき!
I like pasta!

All about
- Food and drinks

Culture
- Japanese food and drinks

Language patterns
- Asking about meals and responding
  あさごはんに　なにを　たべますか。
  あさごはんに　トーストを　たべます。
  オレンジジュースを　のみます。
- Talking about likes and dislikes
  すしが　すき　ですか。
  はい、　だいすき　です。
  はい、　すき　です。
  いいえ、　あんまり。
  いいえ、　きらい　です。
  いいえ、　だいきらい　です。

Text types
- Recipe

Katakana
キ、コ、サ、シ、ソ、タ、チ、ヒ、ミ、ン、ジ、パ、ピ、ン

Unit 7

いつですか
When is it?

All about
- Dates
- Special events

Culture
- Festivals and celebrations in Japan
- School events in Japan

Language patterns
- Asking the day and responding
  きょうは　なん曜日　ですか。
  きょうは　火曜日　です。
- Asking the date and responding
  テストは　なん月　なん日　ですか。
  テストは　四月　十六日　です。
- Asking when an event will take place and responding
  パーティーは　いつ　ですか。
  パーティーは　二月　十一日　です。
  パーティーは　あした　です。
  パーティーは　金曜日　です。

Text types
- Calendar

Katakana
ク、テ、マ、ヤ、レ、

Kanji
日、月、火、水、木、金、土、曜、休

Unit 8

しゅみは?
What are your hobbies?

All about
- Hobbies and interests

Culture
- Traditional sports and cultural activities

Language patterns
- Asking about hobbies and interests and responding
  しゅみは　なん　ですか。
  しゅみは　コンピューター　です。
- Asking about sports and responding
  どんな　スポーツを　しますか。
  ぼくは　ラグビーを　します。
- Talking about what someone can do
  りょうりが　できますか。
  はい、　できます。
  いいえ、　できません。
  すこし、　あまり、　ぜんぜん

Text types
- Interview

Katakana
ツ、ネ、ノ、フ、ホ、ル、ギ、グ、ダ、バ、ボ、ポ

Unit 9

どこに?　だれと?
なんで?
Where to? Who with?
How will you get there?

All about
- Weekend activities

Culture
- Japan's bullet trains

Language patterns
- Asking where someone is going on the weekend and responding
  しゅうまつに　どこに　いきますか。
  うみに　いきます。
- Asking who someone is going with and responding
  だれと　いきますか。
  ゆきさんと　いきます。
- Asking how someone is getting there and responding
  なんで　いきますか。
  バスで　いきます。

Text types
- Text message

Katakana
ウ、セ、ナ、ム、ロ、デ、ド

The Obento song

Verse 1

あ か さ た な は ま
ひらがな、 かたかな
い き し ち に ひ み
ひらがな、 かたかな
あ か さ た な は ま
ひらがな、 かたかな
い き し ち に ひ み
にほんごは すごい

Verse 2

う く す つ ぬ ふ む
ひらがな できる
え け せ て ね へ め
ひらがな できる
う く す つ ぬ ふ む
ひらがな できる
え け せ て ね へ め
ちょっと まって、 あのうね

Chorus

にほんごは たのしい
おべんとうは おいしい
1、2、3、4、5
さあ、 おべんとう
にほんに いきましょう
ともだちに あいましょう
1、2、3、4、5
さあ、 おべんとう

Verse 3

お こ そ と の ほ も
みんな、 おべんとう
にほんご やさしい
みんな、 おべんとう
お こ そ と の ほ も
みんな、 おべんとう
にほんご やさしい
みなさん、 いっしょに!

Ioan-Liviu Orletchi

ISBN 9780170196826

どうぞよろしく

メニュー

Find extra vocabulary on p. 24

01

二

2

どうぞよろしく

ISBN 9780170196826

Have a think

1. How does Ben get everyone's attention?
2. How does Ben address the girls when he calls their names?
3. How does Ben address the boys when he calls their names?
4. Look at the way はい is used. What do you think they mean by はい?
5. Look at the way the students greet each other. How does it compare with how you greet your friends?
6. Imagine you are in Japan. Greet each other and introduce yourself.

01

四

4

どうぞよろしく

ISBN 9780170196826

どんなあじ？

Greeting and saying goodbye

ロールプレー

A	☐さん、	こんにちは。
	☐くん、	おはようございます。
	☐ちゃん、	さようなら。
	☐せんせい、	また あした。
B	☐さん、	こんにちは。
	☐くん、	おはようございます。
	☐ちゃん、	さようなら。
	☐せんせい、	また あした。

ISBN 9780170196826

どうぞよろしく

Asking someone's name and introducing yourself

ロールプレー

A	おなまえは?	
B	☐ です. わたしは ☐ です. ぼくは ☐ です.	どうぞ よろしく.

どうぞよろしく

ISBN 9780170196826

Giving instructions

The せつめい pages at the back of this book will give you even more information to help you talk about greetings, goodbyes, introductions and instructions. Just turn to page 219.

turn to page 219.

ロールプレー

A	☐さん、	☐て　ください。
	☐くん、	

01

七

ISBN 9780170196826

どうぞよろしく

ひらがな
- There are 46 *hiragana* characters.
- *Hiragana* look round and curly.
- *Hiragana* are used to write words originating in Japan.

中山学園学食メニュー
(なか やま がく えん がく しょく)

めん類 (るい)

1
うどん
300円

2
きつねうどん
330円

3
カレーうどん
400円

4
そば
300円

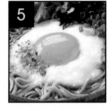
5
月見そば (つきみ)
350円

6
てんぷらそば
400円

7
ラーメン
300円

軽食 (けい しょく)

8
サンドイッチ
350円

9
おにぎり
300円

10
カレーライス
350円

定食 (てい しょく)

11
日替わり定食 (ひ が てい しょく)
500円

12
すし定食 (てい しょく)
450円

漢字 (かん じ)
- *Kanji* look more complicated and have meanings.
- *Kanji* are used to write Japanese words.
- *Kanji* were developed from pictures and symbols.

Photos by Shutterstock.com, Corbis/amanaimages/Gyro Photography, Ioan-Liviu Orletchi, Corbis/Sung-Il, Getty Images, iStockphoto

ISBN 9780170196826

カタカナ

- There are 46 *katakana* characters.
- *Katakana* look straight and pointy.
- *Katakana* are used to write words originating outside of Japan.

ドリンク

13

オレンジジュース
100円

14

アップルジュース
100円

15

ラムネ
100円

16

はちみつレモン
100円

17

コーラ
100円

18

ファンタ
100円

19

ココア
150円

ISBN 9780170196826

Have a think

1 What kind of document is this? How do you know?
2 What do you think the writing under each photo says?
3 What do you think 円 means?
4 What do you notice about the prices on the page?
5 How would you describe the shape of the Japanese characters? Are they all the same shape?
6 How does this canteen menu compare with your school's canteen menu?
7 What would you order for lunch from this menu?
8 If you had to write your school's canteen menu in Japanese, what kind of writing would the items be written in? Why?
9 Do you think that a Japanese-style しょくどう (canteen) would be popular in Australia?

Have a go

1 Imagine you were in charge of your school's canteen. What 日替り定食 (set meal of the day) would you create?
2 Think back to when you were learning to read and write your own language. What strategies did you use to remember how to read and write? Make up a game to practise reading or writing Japanese.

Kanji were developed from pictures and symbols. These examples show the origin and meanings of some *kanji*.

middle	mountain	month or moon	day or sun
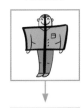			
中	山	月	日

01

九

どうぞよろしく

ひらがな

This is the *hiragana* alphabet. Use the chart to say the sounds. Your teacher will help you.

*	w	r	y	m	h	n	t	s	k		
ん n	わ	ら	や	ま	は	な	た	さ	か	あ	a
	り		み	ひ	に	ち chi	し shi	き	い		i
	る	ゆ	む	ふ fu	ぬ	つ tsu	す	く	う		u
	れ		め	へ	ね	て	せ	け	え		e
	を	ろ	よ	も	ほ	の	と	そ	こ	お	o

Here are the *hiragana* introduced in this unit.

どうぞよろしく

ISBN 9780170196826

Once you can recognise the characters, follow these three steps to read the words:

1 **Look** at the first character of the word.
2 **Think** of a word you know that starts with that character.
3 **Count** the number of characters and see if it matches the word you know. If not, try another word until you find a match.

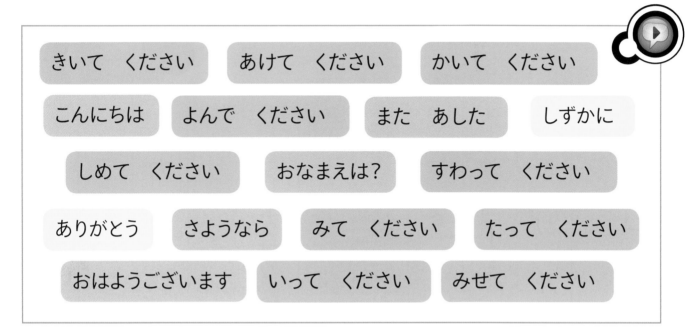

きいて ください　　あけて ください　　かいて ください

こんにちは　よんで ください　　また あした　　しずかに

しめて ください　　おなまえは?　　すわって ください

ありがとう　　さようなら　　みて ください　　たって ください

おはようございます　　いって ください　　みせて ください

たかこ

ゆき

けんいち

ゆうすけ

なかむらせんせい

ISBN 9780170196826

01

+
−

どうぞよろしく

カタカナ

This is the *katakana* alphabet. It has 46 sounds made up of a consonant and a vowel, or just a vowel. Each *hiragana* has a corresponding *katakana* sound.

*	w	r	y	m	h	n	t	s	k		
ン n	ワ	ラ	ヤ	マ	ハ	ナ	タ	サ	カ	ア	**a**
		リ		ミ	ヒ	ニ	チ chi	シ shi	キ	イ	**i**
		ル	ユ	ム	フ fu	ヌ	ツ tsu	ス	ク	ウ	**u**
		レ		メ	ヘ	ネ	テ	セ	ケ	エ	**e**
	ヲ	ロ	ヨ	モ	ホ	ノ	ト	ソ	コ	オ	**o**

Here are the *katakana* introduced in this unit.

ベ be　ヘ he　ハ ha　ト to　ケ ke　エ e

ケイト　　　エマ　　　ベン　　　ハジョーノ　　　トニー

どうぞよろしく

ISBN 9780170196826

Conversation

Have you noticed how often words like 'um', 'hey' and 'er' are used in conversations in English? Similar words are used in Japanese.

Make up a role-play using the language learnt in this unit, and use words such as the following to make it sound more natural.

あのねー
Hey!

あっ！
Oh!

えーと
Let me see (used when thinking)

あのー
Um

ううん
No!

うん
Yeah!

Jack Lewis, Jordan Lewis and Aki Murao-Lewis

Why are these people speaking differently?

せんせい、　おはようございます。

べんくん、　おはよう。

ゆきさん、　おはよう。

けんいちくん、　おはよう。

よし！　おはよう。

やまちゃん、　おはよう。

01

十三

ISBN 9780170196826

Manga

Manga are popular all over the world, not only as comic stories but as an art form. The most distinctive features of Japanese *manga* are their illustrations and the way the text flows from one frame to the next. When *manga* are translated into English, the frames follow a similar order to Japanese. Look at the example below.

Read the *manga* following the arrows.

Notice the sound effects. What are they written in?

Notice the *furigana* beside the *kanji*. Why do you think it is useful?

Notice which words are written in *hiragana*, *katakana* and *kanji*.

Look at the Japanese and the English versions. How do you say 'It's no use!' in Japanese?

どうぞよろしく

ISBN 9780170196826

Create your own *manga*. Brainstorm what you can say in Japanese. Then, write and illustrate your own *manga* using all of the phrases you have learnt so far.

ISBN 9780170196826

01

十
五

どうぞよろしく

ごはんとおかず

ごはん

Alamy

Corbis/amanaimages/Doable

Greeting and saying goodbye

たかこさん、	おはようございます。
<ruby>ハジョーノ<rt>は じょー の</rt></ruby>くん、	こんにちは。
みなさん、	さようなら。
なかむらせんせい、	また　あした。
Takako,	good morning.
Harjono,	hello/good afternoon.
Everyone,	goodbye.
Mr Nakamura,	see you tomorrow.

Asking someone's name and introducing yourself

おなまえは?	
What is your name?	
わたしは	たかこ　です。
ぼくは	ゆうすけ　です。
<ruby>ハジョーノ<rt>は じょー の</rt></ruby>　です。	
I am	Takako.
I am (boys)	Yuusuke.
Harjono.	
どうぞ　よろしく。	
Pleased to meet you.	

Giving instructions

たかこさん、	たって　ください。
<ruby>ハジョーノ<rt>は じょー の</rt></ruby>くん、	よんで　ください。
みなさん、	
なかむらせんせい、	
Takako,	please stand.
Harjono,	please read.
Everyone,	
Mr Nakamura,	

どうぞよろしく

ISBN 9780170196826

おかず

Greeting and saying goodbye

Getty Images

Core

おはようございます	good morning
こんにちは	hello; good afternoon
さようなら	goodbye
また　あした	see you tomorrow
どうぞ　よろしく	pleased to meet you

More

はい	yes
いいえ	no
またね	see you later
おやすみなさい	good night
ありがとう	thank you

Titles

Core

☐ せんせい	(used as a title for teachers and doctors)
☐ さん	(used after any name)
☐ くん	(used after boys' names)
☐ ちゃん	(used after young children's names)

Who?

Core

わたし	I; me
ぼく	I; me (used by boys)
みなさん	everyone

Giving instructions

Core

たって	stand up
すわって	sit down
きいて	listen
みて	look
みせて	show
かいて	write
よんで	read
いって	say
しずかに　して	be quiet
☐ ください	please ☐

More

まどを　あけて	open the window
まどを　しめて	shut the window
ドアを　あけて	open the door
ドアを　しめて	shut the door
まって	wait
ちょっと　まって	wait a minute

01

十
七

テーブルマナー

しゅんくんの一日

Shun is a Japanese boy who lives in Tokyo. This is the true story of a day in Shun's life.

1.6

Fact file

Most Japanese schools have a school uniform. Boys' high school uniforms are often dark, military-style uniforms with a white shirt and a jacket done up to the neck. The buttons have the school emblem on them, and the pin on the collar indicates what year the boy is in.

Girls have dark blue, grey or green suit-style uniforms. Many schools have a uniform in the style of a sailor suit for girls, with white knee-high socks.

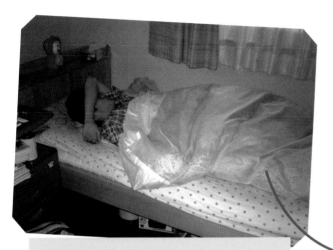

I usually get up around 7 o'clock. When I was little I slept on a ふとん (futon), but now I sleep in a bed, which means that I don't have to fold it up each day and hang it out on the balcony.

I'm half asleep as I put on my shirt. I'm a ちゅうがくさんねんせい (third-year student at junior high, which is equivalent to an Australian Year 9 student) and my uniform is just a shirt and pants.

Fact file

A ふとん (futon) is a Japanese-style bed on the floor. It consists of a しきぶとん (soft mattress), a かけぶとん (quilt) and a まくら (pillow). A ふとん is placed onto the たたみ (floor matting) at night, and is folded away and stored in a cupboard called an おしいれ during the day.

Fact file

Traditional breakfasts consist of steamed rice, miso soup and various side dishes. The side dishes might include grilled fish, たまごやき (omelette), つけもの (pickles), のり (dried seaweed) and salad. This is usually washed down with おちゃ (green tea).

Japanese boys particularly like なっとう, which is sticky fermented soya beans, usually eaten stirred through hot steamed rice.

For breakfast I always have rice with なっとう (fermented beans) and みそしる (miso soup), and some fruit. Then I have a cup of hot milk or おちゃ (green tea).

どうぞよろしく

I walk to school. It takes about 15 minutes. A lot of other kids have to catch the train.

Fact file

Most primary and junior high school students who go to public schools walk or ride bikes to and from school.

Students who go to private schools may need to travel further, so they use crowded trains or buses with rush-hour commuters. They use rechargeable prepaid travel cards, which allow them to travel on buses and trains. They simply hold their cards near the card readers and the travel cost will be deducted from the card. These cards can also be used in some shops. Some mobile phones can also be configured to act as travel cards.

I go to Koganei Junior High School. As soon as we get to school we change our shoes and put on うわばき (indoor shoes or slippers), which we wear inside the school buildings and grounds. We leave our school shoes in the くつばこ (shoe cupboard) and collect them again on the way out.

Fact file

The Japanese school system has six years of しょうがっこう (primary school), three years of ちゅうがっこう (junior high school) and three years of こうこう (senior high school). Then, most students go on to two years of college or four years of だいがく (university).

First lesson is homeroom. We have 40 students in each class, with four classes in each grade. Each lesson goes for 50 minutes and my favourite subjects are PE and Social Studies.

01

All photos by Takeshi, Kyoko and Shun Takahashi

ISBN 9780170196826

十
九

どうぞよろしく

Mum makes the best おべんとう (lunch boxes)! Today it's ごもくごはん (rice) with にもの (simmered chicken and pork), potato salad and すのもの (cucumber in a vinegar dressing). We all sit in the classroom and eat. Sometimes we go to the しょくどう (canteen) and buy カレーライス (curry rice) or ラーメン (noodle soup).

When we were in primary school, we had a hot lunch each day. That's called きゅうしょく.

Fact file

An おべんとう is a Japanese-style lunch box – usually rice and a variety of side dishes, including meat, vegetables, salad, seafood and pickles. Lunch boxes are taken to school or work, often wrapped in ふろしき (wrapping cloths). If you do not have time to make one at home, you can easily buy one at a コンビニ (convenience store) on the way.

At the end of the day, we have to clean our classrooms. It's called そうじ (cleaning). We are allocated areas to clean: the classrooms, the balconies, the corridors. We sweep the floors, and wipe the boards and the shelves.

Fact file

Every day after classes, the students and teachers clean the school together. They sweep the classrooms and hallways, hose down the bathrooms, dust the boards and windows, empty the garbage and separate the recyclables. It generally takes about 20 minutes.

About once a term everyone does a more extensive clean. Students clean the outside areas, and wash windows and stairways.

Fact file

Most students participate in club activities after school. Students have a wide range of options, from music and cultural clubs – like band, choir, tea ceremony and flower arranging – to sporting clubs – like rugby, soccer, baseball, tennis, basketball, volleyball, track and field, and swimming. Another club is the English-speaking club, which is popular in most schools. Clubs do not just practise their sport or activity; they meet on weekends and have parties or go out together.

I'm in the baseball club. We meet after school on Monday, Tuesday, Thursday and Friday.

Now that I'm in third year, I'm a せんぱい (senior) and it's my job to take care of the こうはい (juniors).

When I get home from school, I have a quick snack. My favourite is cup noodles. Then, it's into homework.

We always have lots of homework, not only from school, but from じゅく (tutoring) as well. I go to じゅく four days a week: Tuesday for English, Wednesday for Science and Social Studies, Thursday for Japanese and Saturday for Maths. I don't mind it because I have friends who go as well. Because I'm in my third year, I have to go more often to prepare for the じゅけん (senior high school entrance exams).

Fact file

じゅく are special private schools that offer lessons after school hours and on the weekends. They help students perform better at school or prepare for university or senior high school entrance exams. They offer courses in Japanese, English, Maths, Science and Social Studies. Students can also study musical instruments, art, swimming and abacus. About half of all high school students attend じゅく.

Fact file

Japanese baths are not for washing but for relaxing! You wash yourself thoroughly before getting into the bath. To wash, you use a hand shower or sit on a small stool and wash from a plastic bowl, which is in the ふろば (bathroom). The water in the bath is not changed between bathers, but is kept hot by a thermostat on the wall.

I usually have an おふろ (bath) at around 10 o'clock. The bath is deep and filled with very hot water, so it's great to relax in. I sit in the bath for about half an hour. Sometimes, I nearly go to sleep.

Have a think

1.4

1   What do you think are the advantages and disadvantages of sleeping on a ふとん (futon)? Why do you think they are placed on たたみ (floor matting)?
2   How does the Japanese school uniform compare with your school uniform?
3   Do you have any daily activities at your school that make it different from other schools?
4   Should students have to clean their own school? What do you think?
5   Survey your class to find out what kinds of school lunches are common in Australia today.
6   Does じゅく (tutoring) exist in Australia?
7   How does Shun's week compare with yours? Who is busier?

Have a go

1   Make yourself a Japanese-style bed on the floor at home. Where would be the best place to set up your ふとん (futon)?
2   Find a recipe for miso soup. Try making some and having it for breakfast.
3   Set up a げんかん (entrance) to your classroom. For one week, take off your shoes as you enter the classroom. What are the advantages and disadvantages of changing your shoes?
4   Organise a class debate: Australian students should do そうじ (cleaning) like students in Japan.

01

二
十
一

Hints for learning Japanese

Brainstorm in your class and see if you can come up with other hints for learning Japanese.

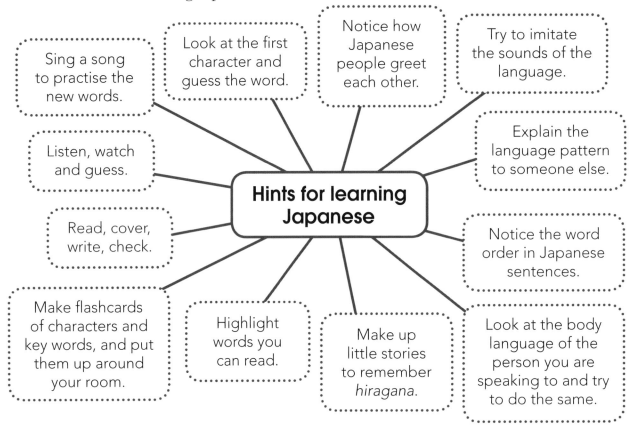

Sing a song to practise the new words.

Look at the first character and guess the word.

Notice how Japanese people greet each other.

Try to imitate the sounds of the language.

Listen, watch and guess.

Explain the language pattern to someone else.

Hints for learning Japanese

Read, cover, write, check.

Notice the word order in Japanese sentences.

Make flashcards of characters and key words, and put them up around your room.

Highlight words you can read.

Make up little stories to remember *hiragana*.

Look at the body language of the person you are speaking to and try to do the same.

Being polite

You can thank people in different ways, depending on how polite you need to be. Consider the different ways that you can say 'thank you' in Japanese.

iStockphoto

Thank you!

more polite

ありがとう　ございます
どうも　ありがとう
ありがとう
どうも

less polite

どうぞよろしく

ISBN 9780170196826

おかし

うたいましょう

Ioan-Liviu Orletchi

♪ The greetings song

Sing this song to the tune of 'Row, Row, Row
Your Boat' to remember the Japanese greetings.

おはようございます、
こんにちは、
さようなら、　みなさん、
また　あした

♪ The stand up, sit down overture

Here is a song that will help you learn the classroom expressions.
It is sung to the tune of the 'Light Cavalry Overture' by Franz von Suppé.

たって、　すわって、　たって、　すわって、
あけて、　しめて
きいて、　みて、　かいて、　よんで、　もういちど　いって

たって、　すわって、　たって、　すわって、
あけて、　しめて
ほんを　だして、　ペンを　かして、　ノートを　みせて

♪ The stand up, sit down rap

As you sing, do the actions.

たって、　すわって
まどを　あけて、　まどを　しめて

たって、　すわって
ドアを　あけて、　ドアを　しめて

たって、　すわって
きいて、　みて、　かいて、　よんで

たって、　すわって
しずかに、　しずかに

かけじく

Ask your teacher
to show you how to
make a かけじく
(Japanese wall hanging).

01

二十三

23

ISBN 9780170196826

どうぞよろしく

かぞえましょう

メニュー

Find extra vocabulary on p. 45

かぞえましょう

ISBN 9780170196826

ISBN 9780170196826

かぞえましょう

もしもし、たかこ　です。

ありがとう、ベンくん。ちょっと　まって!

こんにちは。ベン　です。おたんじょうび　おめでとう!

ベンくん、でんわ　ばんごうは?

042-266-3939　です。

3939…?

ああ、サンキュー　ベリー　マッチ!

Have a think

1 What do the students wear to practise *kendo*?
2 How many strokes did the *kendo* club practise in the first two rounds? How many did they practise in the third round?
3 Look at the way the *kendo* club members thank each other at the end of the session. How does it compare with the way you thank each other at the end of your sports matches?
4 How do you wish someone a happy birthday in Japanese?
5 How do you ask someone's age in Japanese? How old is Takako today?
6 How do you answer the phone in Japanese?
7 What is Ben's phone number?
8 What are the four ways of saying 'thank you' used in this story? How many ways can you say 'thank you' in English? Put your list of words in order of politeness.

かぞえましょう

ISBN 9780170196826

どんなあじ?

Counting to 20

はじめ!
一、二、三、四、五、六、七、八、九、十。
おわり!

はじめ!
一、二、三、四、五、六、七、八、九、十、
十一、十二、十三、十四、十五、十六、
十七、十八、十九、二十。
おわり!

ロールプレー

A	はじめ! 一、二、三、四、五、六、七、八、九、十、十一、十二、十三、十四、十五、十六、十七、十八、十九、二十。 おわり!

ISBN 9780170196826

かぞえましょう

Asking someone's age and responding

かぞえましょう

A	なんさい　ですか。		
B	わたしは ぼくは	☐さい　です。	☐さんは？ ☐くんは？
A	わたしは ぼくは わたしも ぼくも	☐さい　です。	

ISBN 9780170196826

Asking someone's telephone number and responding

The せつめい pages at the back of this book will give you even more information to help you talk about counting, telephone numbers and ages. Just turn to page 220.

Just turn to page 220.

ロールプレー

A	でんわ　ばんごうは？	
	☐さん、	でんわ　ばんごうは？
	☐くん、	
B	☐　です。	
	でんわ　ばんごうは　☐　です。	

つくりましょう！

Sudoku

Yes, sudoku puzzles are Japanese. However, you might be surprised by their history.

1 Do some research online to discover the history of the sudoku puzzle.
2 Try solving a sudoku puzzle.

	一				二		八	三
三				六	五	二	一	
九		七			八			
	六		八			一		四
	九	四		三	五			
八		一			九		七	
			五			四		六
	三	六	二	七				九
四	五		三				二	

Business cards

Japanese people use business cards (めいし) all the time. They contain a person's name and contact details.

　　めいしを　みて　ください! See if you can read the phone numbers on this one.

なかやまがくえん　ぶ
中山学園けんどう部

もりやま　たかこ
森山　高子

東京都国分寺市本田一丁目三十三番五号
でんわ:（〇四二）三五七　〇八三五
Mob:（〇九〇）五四七八　〇三六五
moriyama.takako@docomo.co.jp

かぞえましょう

ISBN 9780170196826

Tallies

| | | || | ||| | |||| | 卌 |

一　丁　下　下　正

Instead of using tally marks, Japanese people use the kanji 正. It means 'correct', has five strokes and is easy to use when counting sets of five.

Kenichi did a survey of the ages of the members of his school soccer club. Here is his tally sheet. Read the table and answer your teacher's questions about the data.

なかやまがくえん　さっかーぶ
中山学園のサッカー部

なんさい　ですか。		
とし		ごうけい
十一さい	正 正 一	十一
十二さい	正 正 正 一	十六
十三さい	正 正 下	十三
十四さい	正 正 正 正 正 下	二十八
十五さい	正 正 正 正 下	二十四
十六さい	正 正 正 下	十九
十七さい	正 正 正 正 下	二十三
十八さい	正 正 正	十五
		百四十九

Ioan-Liviu Orletchi

Have a think

1　How many players are in each age group?
2　How many people in total are in the soccer club?
3　If a soccer team has 11 players, how many teams are in each age group?

ISBN 9780170196826

かぞえましょう

べんきょうのベン

ひらがな

This is the *hiragana* alphabet. Use the chart to say the sounds.
Your teacher will help you.

*	w	r	y	m	h	n	t	s	k		
ん n	わ	ら	や	ま	は	な	た	さ	か	あ	a
	り		み	ひ	に	ち chi	し shi	き	い		i
	る	ゆ	む	ふ fu	ぬ	つ tsu	す	く	う		u
	れ		め	へ	ね	て	せ	け	え		e
を	ろ	よ	も	ほ	の	と	そ	こ	お		o

Here are the *hiragana* introduced in this unit.

 わ wa ほ ho は ha て te

 ぼ bo ば ba で de

かぞえましょう

ISBN 9780170196826

Once you can recognise the characters, follow these three steps to read the words and the sentences:

1 **Look** at the first character of the word or sentence.
2 **Think** of a word you know that starts with that character.
3 **Count** the number of characters and see if it matches the word you know.
   If not, try another word until you find a match.
   Then, keep skim reading through the sentence to find other words you know.

Hey! Did you notice that 'wa' is written as は?

は

Not only does the hard-working は have a role in words like おはよう and はち, but it is also used for the particle that is pronounced 'wa'.

わたし**は**　エマ　です。
わたし**は**　十三さい　です。
ぼく**は**　ベン　です。
ぼく**は**　十四さい　です。

The particle は, 'wa', is a subject marker. It shows the main topic or subject of a sentence or conversation. For example, in the next sentence, it follows the Japanese word for telephone number, showing that the telephone number is the subject of the sentence.

でんわ　ばんごう**は**　九八一六　〇八九〇　です。

In the examples above, it followed わたし and ぼく (I/me), so what do you think was the subject of these sentences?

ISBN 9780170196826

02

三
十
五

35

かぞえましょう

かんじ

Kanji originated in China and were introduced into Japan about 1500 years ago. They evolved from pictures and symbols, or combinations of both.

Whereas *hiragana* and *katakana* are based on sound, *kanji* are based on meaning. *Kanji* are used in combination with *hiragana* and *katakana*. *Kanji* are used for writing the nouns, adjectives, verbs and adverbs, and *hiragana* are used to write the grammatical endings and words that do not have *kanji*.

It is often easier to read a piece of Japanese text with *kanji* in it because you can easily understand the meaning from the *kanji*.

Look at the difference in the two sentences below. They both mean the same thing: 'Hi. I'm Emma. I am 17 years old. My phone number is 9677-8913.'

こんにちは。　わたしは　エマ　です。　じゅうななさい　です。
でんわ　ばんごうは　きゅうろくなななな　はちきゅういちさん　です。

こんにちは。　わたしは　エマ　です。　十七さい　です。
でんわ　ばんごうは　九六七七　八九一三　です。

Kanji numbers

See if you can read these.

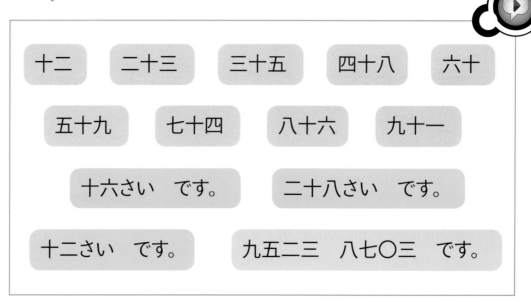

十二　　二十三　　三十五　　四十八　　六十

五十九　　七十四　　八十六　　九十一

十六さい　です。　　二十八さい　です。

十二さい　です。　　九五二三　八七〇三　です。

かぞえましょう

ISBN 9780170196826

Here are some ways to remember the *kanji* for the numbers in Japanese.

one	two	three	four	five
one pencil	two pencils	three pencils	square window with curtains	**go** on a picnic
いち	に	さん	し よん	ご

six	seven	eight	nine	ten
rock star	hug a ba**nana**	rabbit **hutch**	**cu**te baby	**ju**ice
ろく	なな しち	はち	きゅう く	じゅう

三十七

ISBN 9780170196826

かぞえましょう

ごはんとおかず

ごはん

2.4

iStockphoto

Corbis/TW Photo

Counting to 20

はじめ!	一、二、三、四、五、六、七、八、九、十、十一、十二、十三、十四、十五、十六、十七、十八、十九、二十。	おわり!
Start!	1, 2, 3, 4, 5, 6, 7, 8, 9, 10, 11, 12, 13, 14, 15, 16, 17, 18, 19, 20	Finish!

Asking someone's age and responding

なんさい　ですか。
How old are you?
How old is she/he?
十二_{じゅうに}さい　です。 わたしは　十四_{じゅうよん}さい　です。 ぼくも　十四さい　です。
12 years old. I am 14 years old. I am also 14 years old.

十二 (じゅうに) さい　です。
わたしは　十四 (じゅうよん) さい　です。
ぼくも　十四さい　です。

Asking someone's telephone number and responding

でんわ　ばんごうは?
What is your telephone number?
九七六八　一九四五　です。 〇四二　二六六　三九三九　です。
It is 9768-1945. It is 042-266-3939.

ISBN 9780170196826

おかず

Counting to 20

2.5

Core

〇	れい or ゼロ	0
一	いち	1
二	に	2
三	さん	3
四	し or よん	4
五	ご	5
六	ろく	6
七	しち or なな	7
八	はち	8
九	きゅう or く	9
十	じゅう	10
十一	じゅういち	11
十二	じゅうに	12
十三	じゅうさん	13
十四	じゅうし or じゅうよん	14
十五	じゅうご	15
十六	じゅうろく	16
十七	じゅうしち or じゅうなな	17
十八	じゅうはち	18
十九	じゅうきゅう or じゅうく	19
二十	にじゅう	20

Start and finish

More

はじめ	start
おわり	finish

Ages

Core

一さい	いっさい	1 year old
二さい	にさい	2 years old
三さい	さんさい	3 years old
四さい	よんさい	4 years old
五さい	ごさい	5 years old
六さい	ろくさい	6 years old
七さい	ななさい	7 years old
八さい	はっさい	8 years old
九さい	きゅうさい	9 years old
十さい	じゅっさい	10 years old
十一さい	じゅういっさい	11 years old
十二さい	じゅうにさい	12 years old
十三さい	じゅうさんさい	13 years old
十四さい	じゅうよんさい	14 years old
十五さい	じゅうごさい	15 years old
十六さい	じゅうろくさい	16 years old
十七さい	じゅうななさい	17 years old
十八さい	じゅうはっさい	18 years old
十九さい	じゅうきゅうさい	19 years old
二十	はたち	20 years old

Corbis/Bloomimage

02

三十九

ISBN 9780170196826

かぞえましょう

なんさいですか

As well as celebrating birthdays, Japanese people celebrate special ages.

Every year on 15 November, special prayers are offered for children aged 7, 5 and 3 (7-year-old girls, 5-year-old boys and 3-year-old girls – and in some areas 3-year-old boys) to ensure a long and happy life.

Children dress up in formal clothing, many in *kimono*, to visit the local shrine to be blessed. They are given sweets called ちとせあめ (thousand-year candy), which symbolises a long and healthy life.

ちとせあめ

Corbis, Getty Images

しちごさん
七五三

さん
三さい　です。

なな
七さい　です。

ご
五さい　です。

おみやまいり

いっ
一かげつ　です。
(one month old)

Photo Japan/Kenneth Hamm

When a baby is about one month old, parents and grandparents take the child to a Shinto shrine to express gratitude for the baby's safe delivery. The priest prays for the baby's health and happiness.

じゅうさん
十三まいり

Alamy

じゅうさん
十三さい　です。

じゅうさん
十三まいり is a celebration that is popular in the Kansai area (around Osaka and Kyoto) for 13-year-old children. This age is seen as significant as children start their teenage years, when they are faced with the issues of growing up.

Children visit the shrine with their parents to wish for the wisdom to gain their own identity.

かぞえましょう

ISBN 9780170196826

せいじんのひ

はたち
二十です。

AAP Photo/Katsumi Kasahara

The celebrations of long life take place when a person reaches the ages of 60, 70, 77, 80, 88, 90, 99 and then 108. Children and grandchildren – and even great-grandchildren – all gather together and celebrate the person's long life.

ちょうじゅのいわい

はちじゅうはっ
八十八さい　です。

Kouji Fujii

The second Monday in January is せいじんのひ (Coming-of-Age Day). Young people who are turning 20 that year dress in formal clothes and attend a ceremony held at the city hall. Women often wear a long-sleeved *kimono* called a ふりそで.

At the age of 20, a person is granted full rights as an adult. Drinking and smoking are also permitted from this age.

せいじんのひ is a public holiday in Japan.

Have a think ○○○○○○○○○○○○○○○○○○○○○○

1.4

1　Do you think it is a good idea to celebrate these special ages? Why?
2　Do you have similar celebrations in your culture? What do you do?
3　When Japanese people dress up, what do they wear?

Have a go ○○○○○○○○○○○○○○○○○○○○○○

1　Think about the ages and milestones that have been significant in your life. Create a profile that features photos of yourself with information about your age (in Japanese) and the significant events of your life. Show your profile to your class and say your age in Japanese.
2　Do some research to find out more about Japanese traditional clothing or Japanese religion. Report what you learn back to your class.

ISBN 9780170196826

かぞえましょう

おはし

Counting and numbers
Counting on your fingers

Japanese people count on their fingers using only one hand by counting the number of fingers folded down. Look at the diagram and see if you can do it too.

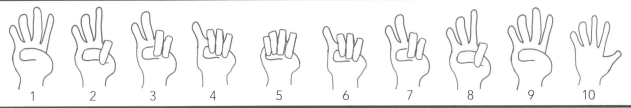

| 1 | 2 | 3 | 4 | 5 | 6 | 7 | 8 | 9 | 10 |

Numbers

Did you notice that Japanese has two words for four, seven and nine?

* four is し or よん.
* seven is なな or しち.
* nine is きゅう or く.

Sometimes you use one and sometimes the other. Your teacher will tell you which to use when. Be careful.

As a general rule, Japanese use よん for four because another word, which is pronounced し, means 'death'. Some superstitious Japanese people believe that the number four is unlucky. They do not like to live at addresses with four in them. Also, if you go to a wedding in Japan, it is traditional to give money to the married couple, but some people consider it bad luck to give an amount of money with a four in it.

Ages

Learning ages in Japanese is not that hard – you follow the pattern of putting さい on the end of the number. However, a few numbers change slightly to make the expression easier to say. The three are:

* 1 year old, いっさい
* 8 years old, はっさい
* 10 years old, じゅっさい

Of course, this pattern follows for other numbers, such as 11, 18, 21, 28 and 30.

Another exception is 20 years old, which is said はたち.

くさい　です!

いいえ、　きゅうさい　です。

はたち
二十　です。

かぞえましょう

ISBN 9780170196826

When you are saying that someone is nine years old, be careful to always use きゅう, as in きゅうさい　です. If you say くさい　です, you are actually saying that the person is smelly!

Kanji or numerals?

Did you know that Japanese people use numerals as well as *kanji*? Of course, numerals are used in maths, phone numbers and dates, but where the writing is written downwards, the numbers are written in *kanji* instead.

Phone numbers

In Japanese phone numbers, the hyphen (-) is very important because it gives information about the area codes. In Japanese, when you say a phone number aloud, you say の whenever a hyphen (or a space) appears in a phone number. The の is not written, it is only said. Mobile phone numbers are the same.

Remember: wherever you see the hyphen (or space), say の.

Talking about others

In the next few units, we are going to learn how to say a lot about ourselves, but it is really easy to say the same things about other people by changing わたし／ぼく(I) to the other person's name, followed by は.

わたしは　十四さい　です。 I am 14 years old.

ケイトさんは　十二さい　です。 Kate is 12 years old.

The question follows the same pattern:

なんさい　ですか。 How old are you?

ケイトさんは　なんさい　ですか。 How old is Kate?

Look at the next two examples. They look the same, don't they? How can that be? Well, in Japanese it is rude to use the word 'you', so when you want to ask someone something about themselves, you use their name as if you were talking about them to someone else.

ケイトさんは　なんさい　ですか。 How old is Kate?

ケイトさんは　なんさい　ですか。 How old are you, Kate?

Getty Images

My phone number, if you were calling me from Australia, would be 0011の (to make an international call) 81の (the country code for Japan) 42の (my area in outer Tokyo, you leave off the 0) 375の (the prefix for my suburb) 6578 (my number).

Getty Images

ISBN 9780170196826

かぞえましょう

うたいましょう

Here is a way to remember the Japanese numbers from 1 to 10 using very silly counting actions and a not so silly counting song. Say the Japanese numbers as you do the actions.

The very silly counting actions

1, 2, itchy, knee (scratch your knee)
3, sun (point to the sun in the sky)
4, yawn (cover your mouth as you yawn) or
4, she (point to a girl in the class)

5, go (point to the door to tell someone to go out)
6, rock (shake your head and play air guitar like a rock star)
7, nana (put your thumbs in your ears and wiggle your fingers and say nah, nah, nanah, nah) or
7, shichi (make your hands like the wheels of a steam train, which sounds like 'shichi shichi shichi shichi')

8, hutch (put your hands above your head like the roof of a rabbit hutch)
9, Q (make the letter Q with your fingers)
10, dew (make the shape of a dew drop with your thumb and pointer finger)

Then, try the same actions while singing the following song to the tune of 'Do Re Mi'. Try to sing the Japanese numbers with the correct pronunciation. Some lines have two versions, depending on which pronunciation you want to remember.

The not so silly counting song

One and two, my いち, に
Three, the さん up in the sky
Four, a よん, I'm really bored, (し, a girl who's in my class)

ご right out the door, bye bye!
ろく, playing my guitar
Seven, なな, nah nah nah (しち, steaming from afar)
Eight the rabbit's はち, and then
きゅう is nine and じゅう is ten

かぞえましょう

ISBN 9780170196826

おしょうゆ

Here are some useful expressions from いただきます.

はじめ!
Start!

おわり!
Finish!

よし!
Well done!

もう いちど!
Once more!

おたんじょうび おめでとう!
Happy birthday!

ちょっと まって!
Just a moment!

うれしい。
Great!

もしもし
Hello (on the phone)

なぁに?
What?

なん ですか。
What is it?

あれは なん ですか。
What is that?

ありがとう
thanks

どうも ありがとう。
thank you

ありがとう ございました
thank you very much

さんきゅー
サンキュー
thank you

どうぞ。
Here you are.

おめでとう! Look at all of the things you have learnt in this unit! Go to your workbook and fill in the checklist at the end of the unit.

¥473

大阪限定

たんじょうび おめでとう

BY KIRAME

02

四十五

45

ISBN 9780170196826

かぞえましょう

Unit 3

どこから？

メニュー

いただきます　47–9

Learn to:
- read a *manga* about people's origins and nationalities
- understand a conversation

どんなあじ？　50–1

Learn to:
- ask where someone comes from and respond
- say your nationality
- ask where someone lives and respond

つくりましょう！　52

Text types:
- self-introduction

べんきょうのベン　53–5

Learn to:
- read the *hiragana* characters と, に, ら, ん and ど
- read the *katakana* characters ア, イ, オ, カ, ス, ニ, ラ, リ and ー
- read the *kanji* characters 日, 本 and 人
- read the words and expressions you will learn in this unit

ごはんとおかず　56–7

Learn about:
- where people live
- where people come from
- countries
- nationalities
- cities

テーブルマナー　58–9

Learn about:
- the map of Japan

おかし　60

Learn to:
- sing a song and perform a rap to help you remember new words

おしょうゆ　61

Learn about:
- other words that will make your Japanese sound natural

Find extra vocabulary on p. 61

ISBN 9780170196826

どこから？

ISBN 9780170196826

1   Harjono is introducing himself. Where is he from? What nationality is he and where does he live?
2   Harjono shows a photo of his friend. What is his friend's name, and where is he from?
3   Where does Harjono's friend live?
4   Where is Emma from? What nationality is she and where does she live?
5   Who are the three people in Emma's photo? Where are they from?
6   How does Tony answer the phone?
7   What does Mr Nakamura ask Tony?
8   けいたいは　だめ！ What school rule does Mr Nakamura remind Tony and Yuusuke? How does this rule apply in your school?

ISBN 9780170196826

どこから？

03

四
十
九

49

どんなあじ?

Asking where someone comes from and responding

カナダ

アメリカ

日本

インドネシア

オーストラリア

ニュージーランド

どこ から きましたか。

インドネシア から きました。

どこ から きましたか。

わたしは ニュージーランド から きました。

どこ から きましたか。

ぼくは オーストラリア から きました。

03

ロールプレー

A	どこ から きましたか。
B	□□ から きました。

五十

50

どこから？

ISBN 9780170196826

Saying your nationality

> にほんじん
> 日本人 です。

> わたしは
> にゅーじーらんどじん
> ニュージーランド人 です。

> おーすとらりあじん
> ぼくは オーストラリア人 です。

ロールプレー

A	☐じん 人 です。

Asking where someone lives and responding

> どこに すんで いますか。

> しどにー
> シドニーに すんで います。

> どこに すんで いますか。

> とうきょうに すんで います。

> どこに すんで いますか。

> にゅーじーらんど
> ニュージーランドに
> すんで います。

ロールプレー

A	どこに すんで いますか。
B	☐に すんで います。

ISBN 9780170196826

つくりましょう！

3.5, 3.6

Self-introduction

When you meet a group of people in Japan, you will often need to introduce yourself in Japanese. If you are meeting a group informally, the じこしょうかい (self-introduction) can be short and simple. If the occasion is more formal – like meeting teachers and students at a school in Japan – you might want to say more.

一だん Level 1

みなさん、　こんにちは。
わたしは　[name]　です。
[Age] さい　です。
わたしは　country 人　です。
わたしは　state/city　から　きました。
city/suburb　に　すんで　います。
でんわ　ばんごうは　[telephone number]　です。
どうぞ　よろしく。

二だん Level 2

みなさん、　こんにちは。　きいて　ください。
ぼくは　[school]　の　[name]　です。
[Age] さい　です。
でんわ　ばんごうは　[telephone number]　です。
わたしは　country 人　です。
わたしは　state/city　から　きました。
City の　suburb　に　すんで　います。
みなさん、　どうぞ　よろしく。

Corbis/Bloomimage

Getty Images

です

Did you notice another important word – です? This word can be used to say many things, such as 'it is', 'I am', 'this is' and 'it has'. See how many things you can say with です already!

の

Because the group you come from is also important in Japanese, じこしょうかい often include the belonging word の. It allows you to give more detail about where you are from. You can include things like:

わたしは　なかやまがくえん**の**　まつだ　ゆき　です。
I am Yuki Matsuda from Nakayama Gakuen.

日本（にほん）**の**　とうきょう　から　きました。
I come from Tokyo, Japan.

とうきょう**の**　しぶやに　すんで　います。
I live in Shibuya in Tokyo.

03

五十二

52

どこから？

ISBN 9780170196826

ひらがな

Use the chart to say the *hiragana* sounds. Your teacher will help you.

*	w	r	y	m	h	n	t	s	k	
ん n	わ	ら	や	ま	は	な	た	さ	か	あ	a
		り		み	ひ	に	ち chi	し shi	き	い	i
		る	ゆ	む	ふ fu	ぬ	つ tsu	す	く	う	u
		れ		め	へ	ね	て	せ	け	え	e
	を	ろ	よ	も	ほ	の	と	そ	こ	お	o

Here are the *hiragana* introduced in this unit.

 ど do ん n ら ra に ni と to

Then, use the look, think and count method to see if you can read the sentences.

どこ から きましたか。　日本 から きました。

せんだい から きました。　オーストラリア から きました。

どこに すんで いますか。　ならに すんで います。

よこはまに すんで います。　おおさかに すんで います。

03

五十三

カタカナ

Use the chart to say the *katakana* sounds. Your teacher will help you.

*	w	r	y	m	h	n	t	s	k		
ン n	ワ	ラ	ヤ	マ	ハ	ナ	タ	サ	カ	ア	a
		リ		ミ	ヒ	ニ	チ chi	シ shi	キ	イ	i
		ル	ユ	ム	フ fu	ヌ	ツ tsu	ス	ク	ウ	u
		レ		メ	ヘ	ネ	テ	セ	ケ	エ	e
	ヲ	ロ	ヨ	モ	ホ	ノ	ト	ソ	コ	オ	o

Here are the *katakana* introduced in this unit.

 ス su   カ ka   オ o   イ i   ア a

 ー
This is a special character that is used to make a vowel sound longer.

 リ ri   ラ ra   ニ ni

Use the look, think and count method to see if you can read these countries' names.

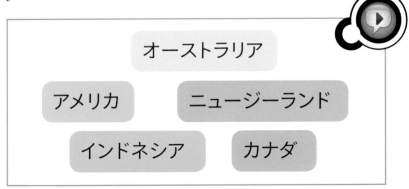

オーストラリア

アメリカ　　ニュージーランド

インドネシア　　カナダ

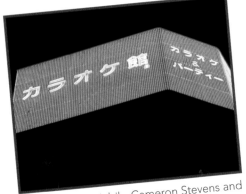

Magdy Habib, Cameron Stevens and Christopher Kocx

ISBN 9780170196826

かんじ

How do you write 'Japan' in *kanji*?

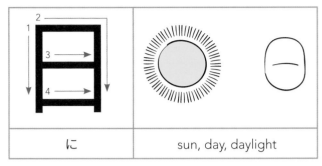

に	sun, day, daylight

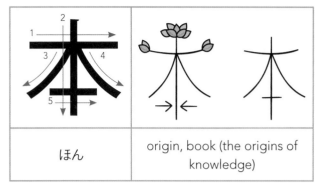

ほん	origin, book (the origins of knowledge)

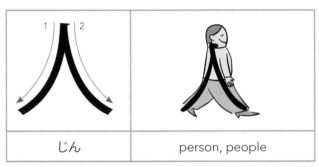

じん	person, people

Each *kanji* has a meaning based on a picture or symbol.

日
sun, day

本
origin, book

人
person

Kanji can be combined to create words with new meanings:

- 日本, Japan (the land where the sun originates)
- 日本人, Japanese people.

Sometimes the pronunciation or reading of a *kanji* changes, depending on the characters it is combined with.

The characters in *kanji* are made up of lines that are called strokes. When writing *kanji*, it is very important to write the strokes in the correct order. The correct stroke order helps you to write smoothly and makes your writing look authentically Japanese.

What do you think the following *kanji* mean? Check your answers at the bottom of this page.

1　日本　　　　　3　オーストラリア人　　　5　三日
2　日本人　　　　4　五人

The small *hiragana* characters placed above *kanji* are called *furigana*. Their job is to help you pronounce the *kanji*.

1 Japan, 2 Japanese people, 3 Australian people, 4 five people, 5 three days

03

五十五

ISBN 9780170196826

どこから？

ごはん

Asking where someone comes from and responding

どこ から きましたか。	ニュージーランド から きました。 日本 から きました。
Where are you from?	I am from New Zealand. I am from Japan.

Saying your nationality

日本人 オーストラリア人 インドネシア人	です。
I am	Japanese. Australian. Indonesian.

Asking where someone lives and responding

どこに すんで いますか。	
Where do you live?	
わたしは ぼくは	とうきょうに すんで います。 おおさかに すんで います。
I	live in Tokyo. live in Osaka.

Magdy Habib, Cameron Stevens and Christopher Kocx

Magdy Habib, Cameron Stevens and Christopher Kocx

The せつめい pages at the back of this book will give you even more information to help you talk about where you are from, nationalities and where you live. Just turn to page 222.

ISBN 9780170196826

おかず

Countries

Core

おーすとらりあ オーストラリア	Australia
に ほん 日本	Japan
いんどねしあ インドネシア	Indonesia
にゅーじーらんど ニュージーランド	New Zealand
か な だ カナダ	Canada
あめりか アメリカ	USA (America)

Asking where someone lives and responding

Ask your teacher how to write and say the name of your city or suburb.

More

じゃ かる た ジャカルタ	Jakarta
お ー くらんど オークランド	Auckland
と ろんと トロント	Toronto
にゅーよーく ニューヨーク	New York
ぱ ー す パース	Perth
し ど に ー シドニー	Sydney
める ほ るん メルボルン	Melbourne
あ で れ ー ど アデレード	Adelaide
ほ ば ー と ホバート	Hobart
ぶ り す べ ん ブリスベン	Brisbane
だ ー ぅぃん ダーウィン	Darwin

Saying your nationality

Core

お ー すとらりあ じん オーストラリア人	Australian
にほんじん 日本人	Japanese
いんどねしあじん インドネシア人	Indonesian
にゅーじーらんどじん ニュージーランド人	New Zealander
か な だ じん カナダ人	Canadian
あ めり か じん アメリカ人	American

Core

とうきょう	Tokyo
きょうと	Kyoto
おおさか	Osaka

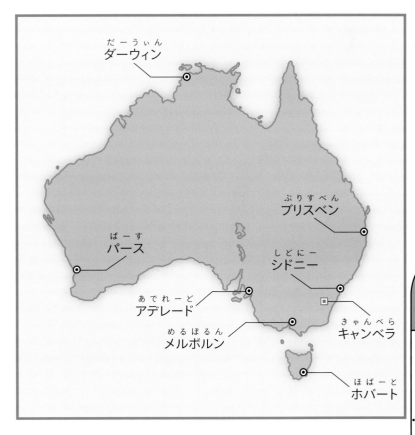

ISBN 9780170196826

03

五十七

57

どこから？

おきなわ
Okinawa

なごや
Nagoya

きょうと
Kyoto

こうべ
Kobe

ひろしま
Hiroshima

ふくおか
Fukuoka

なら
Nara

きゅうしゅう
Kyushu

しこく
Shikoku

おおさか
Osaka

かごしま
Kagoshima

まつやま
Matsuyama

03

五十八

58

どこから?

ISBN 9780170196826

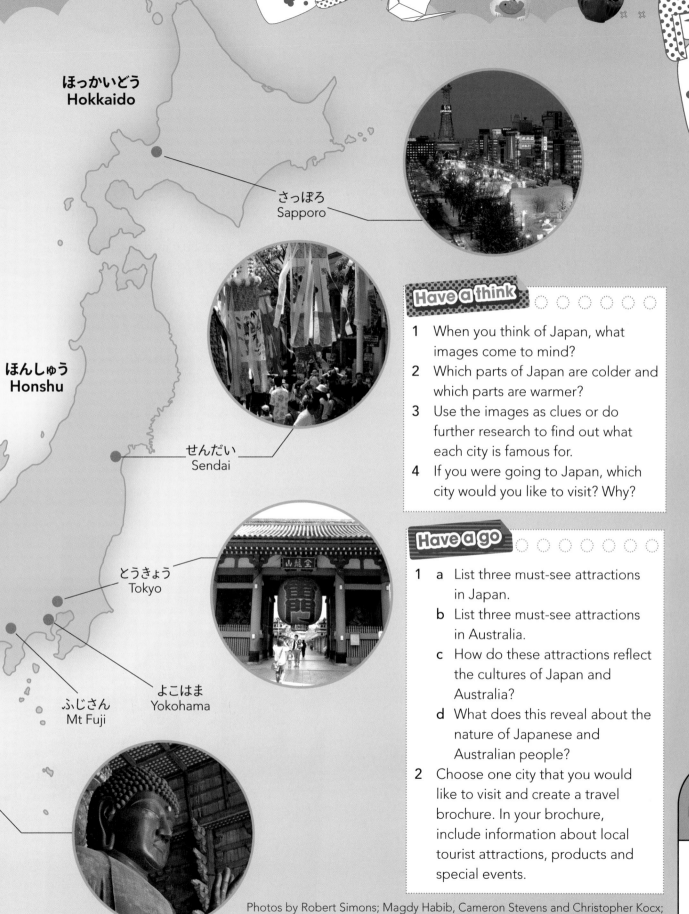

ほっかいどう
Hokkaido

さっぽろ
Sapporo

ほんしゅう
Honshu

せんだい
Sendai

とうきょう
Tokyo

よこはま
Yokohama

ふじさん
Mt Fuji

Have a think ○ ○ ○ ○ ○ ○

1 When you think of Japan, what images come to mind?
2 Which parts of Japan are colder and which parts are warmer?
3 Use the images as clues or do further research to find out what each city is famous for.
4 If you were going to Japan, which city would you like to visit? Why?

Have a go ○ ○ ○ ○ ○ ○

1 a List three must-see attractions in Japan.
   b List three must-see attractions in Australia.
   c How do these attractions reflect the cultures of Japan and Australia?
   d What does this reveal about the nature of Japanese and Australian people?
2 Choose one city that you would like to visit and create a travel brochure. In your brochure, include information about local tourist attractions, products and special events.

03

五十九

59

ISBN 9780170196826

どこから？

うたいましょう

____から きました

Form two teams – the second team echoes the first. The teams then swap roles. You can change the place names to any cities or countries you like.

All: から きました。 (5 claps)
All: から きました。 (5 claps)

Team 1:   どこ から きま した か。
Team 2:   どこ から きま した か。

Team 1:   Hey! Sydney!
Team 2:   Hey! Sydney!

Team 1:   Sydney から きま し た。
Team 2:   Sydney から きま し た。

Team 1:   Hey! Melbourne!
Team 2:   Hey! Melbourne!

Team 1:   Melbourne から きま し た。
Team 2:   Melbourne から きま し た。

Team 1:   Hey! Brisbane!
Team 2:   Hey! Brisbane!

Team 1:   Brisbane から きま し た。
Team 2:   Brisbane から きま し た。

Team 1:   Hey! Perth!
Team 2:   Hey! Perth!

Team 1:   Perth から きま し た。
Team 2:   Perth から きま し た。

Team 1:   Hey! Stop!
Team 2:   Hey! Stop!

All: から きました。 (5 claps)
All: から きました。 (5 claps)
All: から きました。 shshshshshshshsh

____に すんで います

Sing this to the following beat: boom.snap.clap..b.boom.snap.clap.snap boom.snap.clap..b.boom.snap.clap.
    Add your city and your suburb, but don't forget to keep the beat!

どこに すんで いますか。
Sydneyに すんで います

どこに すんで いますか。
Bondiに すんで います

どこに すんで いますか。
Melbourneに すんで います

どこに すんで いますか。
Footscrayに すんで います

Ioan-Liviu Orletchi

どこから?

ISBN 9780170196826

SG 3.6

Here are some useful expressions from いただきます.

だれ ですか。
Who is it/he/she?

これは ぼくの／わたしの
ともだち です。
This is my friend.
ともだち
friend

へえー？
Really?

つぎは エマさん です。
Next is Emma.

なまえは なん ですか。
What is your/his/her name?

だめ ですよ!
It is not allowed!
だめ!
No!
けいたいは だめ!
Mobile phones are not allowed!

あっ! すみません。
Oh, sorry.

けいたい でんわを ください!
Your mobile phone, please!

おめでとう! Look at all of the things you have learnt in this unit! Go to your workbook and fill in the checklist at the end of the unit.

03

ISBN 9780170196826

どこから？

Unit 4

かぞく

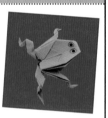

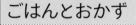

いただきます

かぞく ゲームの じかん です。

It's the ぶんかさい, the cultural festival at school. Ben is the compere for the game show.

チャンキーチャレンジ かぞくゲーム

ケイト　ハジョーノ　ゆうすけ

イェーイ!!!

ゲストは ケイトさん、 ハジョーノくん、 ゆうすけくん です。

Find extra vocabulary on p. 76

1 みなさん、 こんにちは。 ぼくは トニー です。 カナダ から きました。 四人 かぞく です。 おかあさんと、 おとうさんと、 いもうとと、 ぼく です。 ペットが います。 いぬ です。

じゃ、 みなさん、 ビデオを みて ください。 トニーくんの かぞく です。

はい、 トニーくん、 ありがとう。 つぎは エマさん です。

みなさん、 こんにちは。 わたしは エマ です。 ニュージーランド から きました。 六人 かぞく です。 おかあさんと、 おとうさんと、 おばあさんと、 おにいさんと、 いもうとと、 わたし です。 ペットが います。 へび です。

2

04

六十三

63

ISBN 9780170196826

かぞく

かぞく

ISBN 9780170196826

ISBN 9780170196826

かぞく

Have a think

1　How many people are in Tony's family and who are they?
2　How many people are in Emma's family and who are they?
3　What was Ben's first question?
4　What was Ben's next question?
5　What does the machine say when a wrong answer is given?
6　What does the machine say when a correct answer is given?
7　Who won the game?

どんなあじ?

Asking how many people are in someone's family and responding

なん人 かぞく ですか。

八人 です。

六人 です。

四人 です。

Saying who is in your family

おとうさんと　おかあさんと　おじいさんと　おばあさんと　おにいさんと　いもうとと　おとうとと　ぼく　です。

おとうさんと　おかあさんと　おばあさんと　おにいさんと　いもうとと　わたしです。

おとうさんと　おかあさんと　いもうとと　ぼく　です。

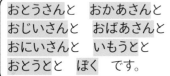

ロールプレー

A	なん人　かぞく　ですか。			
B	□人　です。	□と　□と	わたし　です。 ぼく　です。	□さんは? □くんは?
A	□人　です。	□と　□と	わたし　です。 ぼく　です。	

かぞく

ISBN 9780170196826

4.2

Asking someone if they have any pets and responding

ペット_{べっと}が　いますか。

はい、　います。

ペット_{べっと}が　いますか。

いいえ、　いません。

ペット_{べっと}が　いますか。

はい、　うさぎが　います。

ペット_{べっと}が　いますか。

いいえ、　ペット_{べっと}が　いません。

ペット_{べっと}が　いますか。

はい、　いぬと　ねこが　います。

The せつめい pages at the back of this book will give you even more information to help you talk about family members and pets. Just turn to page 222.

ロールプレー

A	ペット_{べっと}が　いますか。	
B	はい、　□□が　います。 はい、　□と　□が　います。 いいえ、　いません。	□さんは? □くんは?
A	□が　います。 □と　□が　います。 いいえ、　いません。	

04

六十七

······

67

ISBN 9780170196826

つくりましょう！

Family profile

Asuka has written a profile of her family. You can use it as a model to write your own family profile by replacing the words in green with your own information and attaching your own photos.

わたしの　かぞく

こんにちは。　わたしは　おおたに　あすか
です。　十六さい　です。

日本人（にほんじん）　です。　とうきょうに
すんで　います。

わたしは　六人（ろくにん）かぞく　です。　おとうさんと
おかあさんと　おじいさんと　おばあさんと
いもうとと　わたし　です。

ペット（ぺっと）も　います。　ペット（ぺっと）は　いぬです。
いぬが　二（に）ひき　います。　なまえは
ハニー（はにー）と　ペペ（ぺぺ）　です。
ハニー（はにー）は　八（はっ）さい　です。　かわいい　です。
ペペ（ぺぺ）は　十一（じゅういっ）さい　です。　おおきい　です。

ISBN 9780170196826

おとうさんの　なまえは　ただかず
です。　四十五さい　です。
おかあさんの　なまえは　るみこ
です。　四十四さい　です。

いもうとの　なまえは　みお　です。
十三さい　です。

おばあさんの　なまえは　けいこ
です。　七十四さい　です。
おじいさんの　なまえは　かおる
です。　おじいさんも　七十四さい
です。

わたしの　かぞく　です。
どうぞ　よろしく。

ISBN 9780170196826

べんきょうのベン

ひらがな

Use the chart to say the *hiragana* sounds. Your teacher will help you.

*	w	r	y	m	h	n	t	s	k	
ん n	わ	ら	や	ま	は	な	た	さ	か	あ **a**
		り		み	ひ	に	ち chi	し shi	き	い **i**
		る	ゆ	む	ふ fu	ぬ	つ tsu	す	く	う **u**
		れ		め	へ	ね	て	せ	け	え **e**
	を	ろ	よ	も	ほ	の	と	そ	こ	お **o**

Here are the *hiragana* introduced in this unit.

Then, use the look, think and count method to see if you can read these words and sentences.

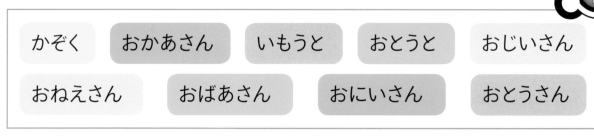

| かぞく | おかあさん | いもうと | おとうと | おじいさん |

おねえさん　　おばあさん　　おにいさん　　おとうさん

ISBN 9780170196826

カタカナ

Use the chart to say the *katakana* sounds. Your teacher will help you.

*	w	r	y	m	h	n	t	s	k		
ン n	ワ	ラ	ヤ	マ	ハ	ナ	タ	サ	カ	ア	a
		リ		ミ	ヒ	ニ	チ chi	シ shi	キ	イ	i
		ル	ユ	ム	フ fu	ヌ	ツ tsu	ス	ク	ウ	u
		レ		メ	ヘ	ネ	テ	セ	ケ	エ	e
	ヲ	ロ	ヨ	モ	ホ	ノ	ト	ソ	コ	オ	o

Here is the *katakana* introduced in this unit.

かんじ

You can write about different numbers of people by combining the *kanji* for the numbers with the character for 'people'. Numbers of people are written like this.

1 person	2 people	3 people	4 people	5 people
一人 ひとり	二人 ふたり	三人 さんにん	四人 よにん	五人 ごにん
6 people	7 people	8 people	9 people	10 people
六人 ろくにん	七人 しちにん ななにん	八人 はちにん	九人 きゅうにん	十人 じゅうにん

See if you can read these.
1 五人　かぞく　です。
2 いもうとが　二人　います。
3 四人　かぞく　です。
4 おにいさんが　三人　います。

1 I have five people in my family. 2 I have two younger sisters. 3 I have four people in my family. 4 I have three older brothers.

ISBN 9780170196826

ごはんとおかず

ごはん

Corbis/Ronnie Kaufman/Larry Hirshowitz

Asking how many people are in someone's family and responding

なん人 かぞく ですか。
How many people are in your family?
五人 です。 六人 です。
There are five people. There are six people.

Saying who is in your family

おとうさんと おかあさんと おばあさんと おにいさんと いもうとと ぼく です。 おかあさんと おじいさんと おねえさんと おとうとと わたし です。
There are my father, mother, grandmother, older brother, younger sister and me. There are my mother, grandfather, older sister, younger brother and me.

Asking someone if they have any pets and responding

You can also use this pattern to ask if someone has a particular relative in their family.

ペットが いますか。	おにいさんが いますか。
Do you have any pets?	Do you have an older brother?
いいえ、 いません。 はい、 へびが います。	いいえ、 いません。 はい、 おにいさんが います。
No, I do not have (any). Yes, I have a snake.	No, I do not. Yes, I have an older brother.

ISBN 9780170196826

おかず

Counting people

なん人	なんにん	How many people?
一人	ひとり	1 person
二人	ふたり	2 people
三人	さんにん	3 people
四人	よにん	4 people
五人	ごにん	5 people
六人	ろくにん	6 people
七人	しちにん／ななにん	7 people
八人	はちにん	8 people
九人	きゅうにん	9 people
十人	じゅうにん	10 people

Family members

Core

かぞく	family
おじいさん	grandfather
おばあさん	grandmother
おとうさん	father
おかあさん	mother
おにいさん	older brother
おねえさん	older sister
おとうと	younger brother
いもうと	younger sister
わたし／ぼく	me
あかちゃん	baby

Pets

Core

ペット	pet
あひる	duck
いぬ	dog
うさぎ	rabbit
うま	horse
きんぎょ	goldfish
とり	bird
ねこ	cat
へび	snake

When you combine the *kanji* for numbers and people, the pronunciation changes for one person and two people, so you have to remember how to say these!

Did you notice that the Japanese words for older members of a family start with お and end with さん to show respect?
Did you also notice ちゃん in あかちゃん? ちゃん is used for someone young (or cute) to show affection.

04

七十三

ISBN 9780170196826

かぞく

テーブルマナー

なんにんかぞくですか

Corbis/Sygma/Noboru Hashimoto

さんにん
三人　かぞく　です。
おとうさんと　おかあさんと
わたし　です。
おとうさんは　すもうの
ちゃんぴおん
チャンピオン　です。

ぼくは　りょうた　です。
よこはまに　すんで　います。
よにん
四人　かぞく　です。おとうさんと
おかあさんと　おねえさんと　ぼく
です。おねえさんは　二十　です。
はたち
ペっと
ペットは　かめ　です。

Markane Sipraseuth

よにん
四人　かぞく　です。
おとうさんと　おかあさんと
いもうと　ぼく　です。
ひろしまに　すんで　います。

Have a think

1　All families are different. Who is in yours?
2　Guess the occupation of the parents in each of the photos. How would the parents' occupation influence the daily life of each family? How might their family life compare with yours?
3　In what way are you influenced by your family?

Have a go

1　Use your family photos or a photo of a famous family to create a family profile in Japanese. Use the language patterns on pages 68–9 as a guide.

かぞく

ISBN 9780170196826

おかし

うたいましょう

Both of the songs on this page can be sung to the tune of 'Ten Little Indians'.

じゅうにん　いますよ

ひとり、　ふたり、　さんにん　います。
よにん、　ごにん、　ろくにん　います。
しちにん、　はちにん、　きゅうにん　います。
じゅうにん　いますよ。

なんにん　かぞく　ですか

おにいさん、　おねえさん、　おとうさん、　おかあさん
いもうと、　おとうと、　おじいさん、　おばあさん
みんなで、　きゅうにん
わたしの　かぞく
なんにん　かぞく　ですか。

Origami

Getty Images

Ask your teacher how to make an origami rabbit.

ISBN 9780170196826

SG 4·6

Here are some useful expressions from いただきます.

かぞく　ゲームの　じかん　です。
It's time for the family game show.

つぎ
next

けすと
ゲスト
guest

ざんねん　ですね。
Bad luck, isn't it?
That's a pity, isn't it?

ああ、　じかん　です。
Oh, your time is up!

いいえ、　ちがいます。
No, that's not right.

はい、　そう　です。
Yes, that's right.
Yes, that's so.

しつもん　です。
Here is the question.

つぎの　しつもん　です。
Here is the next question.

ぜろ
ゼロ
zero

じゅっ
十てん
10 points

また　十てん
another 10 points

すごーい!
Wow!
Incredible!

おめでとう! Look at all of the things you have learnt in this unit! Go to your workbook and fill in the checklist at the end of the unit.

縁結び

ちゃんぴおん　けいと
チャンピオンは　ケイトさん　です。
The champion is Kate.

おめでとう!
Congratulations! (informal)

おめでとう　ございます。
Congratulations! (polite)

ISBN 9780170196826

ワンワン、ガーガー

メニュー

Find extra vocabulary on p. 94

いただきます

05

七十八

ISBN 9780170196826

ISBN 9780170196826

ワンワン、ガーガー

5.1

Have a think 〇〇〇〇〇〇〇〇〇〇〇〇〇〇〇〇〇〇〇〇〇

1 What is said about Kenichi's pet?
2 What is said about Kate's pet?
3 What is said about Emma's pet?
4 Whose pets cause all the commotion?
5 Why does Yuusuke say ひどーい?
6 Describe what happened in the end.
7 Every year in Japan, the third week in September is どうぶつあいごしゅうかん
   (Animal Welfare Week), which is a national community awareness event.
   What similar school or community events do you participate in?

ワンワン、ガーガー

ISBN 9780170196826

5.6

My ideal pet

Create a poster or a PowerPoint presentation about your ideal pet.

Give your work the title わたしの ペット.

You have already learnt enough to include the following information about your ideal pet:

1 the type of pet
2 the pet's name
3 the pet's age
4 a description of the pet
5 where the pet lives
6 what it eats
7 what it drinks.

You can extend yourself by using the following words to start your sentences. (Starting a sentence with 'and' is okay in Japanese.)

そして　　　　and
それから　　　and then
でも　　　　　but
ときどき　　　sometimes

Once you have finished, present your poster or PowerPoint presentation to the class.

05

八十一

ISBN 9780170196826

ワンワン、ガーガー

どんなあじ?

Asking what someone's pet is and responding

ロールプレー

A	ペットは　なん　ですか。
B	ペットは　☐　です。　なまえは　☐　です。

ワンワン、ガーガー

ISBN 9780170196826

Asking whose pet it is and describing pets

だれの ペット ですか。

ゆきさんの ペット です。

かわいい です。

Miniショップ

だれの ペット ですか。

ゆうすけくんの ペット です。

おおきい です。

だれの ペット ですか。

エマさんの へび です。

へびは こわい です。

ロールプレー			
A	だれの ペット ですか。		
B	☐の ペット です。 ☐の ☐ です。	☐ です。 ☐は ☐ です。	

ISBN 9780170196826

ワンワン、ガーガー

Asking what pets eat and drink and responding

5.4

うさぎは　なにを　たべますか。

うさぎは　えさを　たべます。

いぬは　なにを　たべますか。

いぬは　にくを　たべます。

ねこは　なにを　のみますか。

ねこは　みずを　のみます。

ロールプレー

A	☐は　なにを　たべますか。
B	☐を　たべます。
	☐は　☐を　たべます。
A	なにを　のみますか。
	☐は　なにを　のみますか。
B	☐を　のみます。
	☐は　☐を　のみます。

The せつめい pages at the back of this book will give you even more information to help you talk about pets. Just turn to page 223.

ワンワン、ガーガー

ISBN 9780170196826

べんきょうのベン

ひらがな

Use the chart to say the *hiragana* sounds. Your teacher will help you.

*	w	r	y	m	h	n	t	s	k	
ん n	わ	ら	や	ま	は	な	た	さ	か	あ a
		り		み	ひ	に	ち chi	し shi	き	い i
		る	ゆ	む	ふ fu	ぬ	つ tsu	す	く	う u
		れ		め	へ	ね	て	せ	け	え e
	を	ろ	よ	も	ほ	の	と	そ	こ	お o

Here are the *hiragana* introduced in this unit.

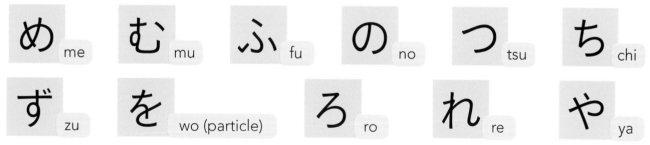

め me　む mu　ふ fu　の no　つ tsu　ち chi
ず zu　を wo (particle)　ろ ro　れ re　や ya

Then, use the look, think and count method to see if you can read these words and sentences.

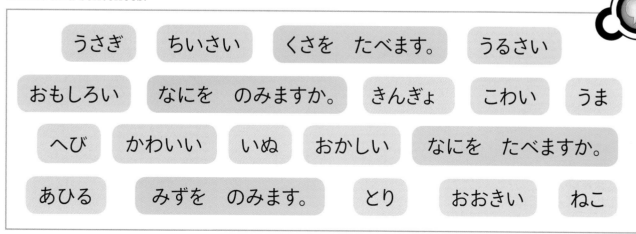

うさぎ　ちいさい　くさを　たべます。　うるさい

おもしろい　なにを　のみますか。　きんぎょ　こわい　うま

へび　かわいい　いぬ　おかしい　なにを　たべますか。

あひる　みずを　のみます。　とり　おおきい　ねこ

05

八十五

85

ISBN 9780170196826

ワンワン、ガーガー

Sound changes

Two symbols are added to certain rows of the *hiragana* table to slightly change the character's sound. They are ° *maru* and ゛ *nigori*, which is also known as *tenten*.

p	b	h	d	t	z	s	g	k	
ぱ pa	ば ba	は ha	だ da	た ta	ざ za	さ sa	が ga	か ka	a
ぴ pi	び bi	ひ hi	ぢ ji	ち chi	じ ji	し shi	ぎ gi	き ki	i
ぷ pu	ぶ bu	ふ fu	づ dzu	つ tsu	ず zu	す su	ぐ gu	く ku	u
ぺ pe	べ be	へ he	で de	て te	ぜ ze	せ se	げ ge	け ke	e
ぽ po	ぼ bo	ほ ho	ど do	と to	ぞ zo	そ so	ご go	こ ko	o

Combination sounds

If you look at a page written in Japanese, you will see the characters や, ゆ and よ sometimes written in smaller type than other characters around them, for example よ (normal) and ょ (small). The small や, ゆ and よ enable us to write combination sounds, like 'sha', 'shu', 'sho', 'kya', 'kyu', 'kyo', 'cha', 'chu' and 'cho'.

r	m	p	
り ri	み mi	ぴ pi	
りゃ rya	みゃ mya	ぴゃ pya	
りゅ ryu	みゅ myu	ぴゅ pyu	
りょ ryo	みょ myo	ぴょ pyo	

What about punctuation?

Punctuation commonly used in Japanese sentences includes:

、	てん	(comma)
。	まる	(full stop)
「 」	かぎかっこ	(quotation marks)

When questions do not end with か, a question mark can be used.

おなまえは?

でんわ　ばんごうは?

八
十
六

ワンワン、ガーガー

ISBN 9780170196826

In modern Japanese, ぢ is replaced by じ, and づ is replaced by ず. Therefore, ぢ and づ are not used very often.

Why are the long 'o' sounds in *hiragana* written with う?

Most words with a long 'o' sound are written with an う, like:

とうきょう	Tokyo
おべんとう	packed lunch
さようなら	goodbye

However, not all of them are. Some words have a long 'o' sound and are written with an お, like:

おおさか	Osaka
とおり	path

Why do some words end with a small っ?

The small っ in words like あっ! and えっ! has the effect of shortening the sound and emphasising that it is an exclamation. This is important when words are used to show surprise.

b	h	n	ch	j	sh	g	k	
び bi	ひ hi	に ni	ち chi	じ ji	し shi	ぎ gi	き ki	
びゃ bya	ひゃ hya	にゃ nya	ちゃ cha	じゃ ja	しゃ sha	ぎゃ gya	きゃ kya	や
びゅ byu	ひゅ hyu	にゅ nyu	ちゅ chu	じゅ ju	しゅ shu	ぎゅ gyu	きゅ kyu	ゆ
びょ byo	ひょ hyo	にょ nyo	ちょ cho	じょ jo	しょ sho	ぎょ gyo	きょ kyo	よ

05

八十七

ISBN 9780170196826

ワンワン、ガーガー

ごはんとおかず

ごはん

Corbis/Hamyoshi Yamaguchi

Asking what someone's pet is and responding

ペットは　なん　ですか。
What pet do you have?
いぬ　です。 ペットは　ねこ　です。
A dog. My pet is a cat.

Asking whose pet it is and describing pets

だれの　ペット　ですか。 だれの　へび　ですか。
Whose pet is it? Whose snake is it?
わたしの　ペット　です。 わたしの　へび　です。 エマさんの　へび　です。
It is my pet. It is my snake. It is Emma's snake.
かわいい　です。 うまは　おおきい　です。
It is cute. The horse is big.

Asking what pets eat and drink and responding

うさぎは　なにを　たべますか。 ねこは　なにを　のみますか。
What do rabbits eat? What do cats drink?
えさを　たべます。 みずを　のみます。
They eat pet food. They drink water.

ワンワン、ガーガー

ISBN 9780170196826

おかず

5.5

Pets

Core

きんぎょ	goldfish
へび	snake
うま	horse
いぬ	dog
うさぎ	rabbit
とり	bird
ねこ	cat
あひる	duck

Adjectives

Core

うるさい	noisy
かわいい	cute
ちいさい	small
おおきい	big
こわい	scary
おもしろい	interesting; funny
すごい	amazing
おかしい	funny; strange
くさい	smelly

More

かわいい	ですね。	It is cute, isn't it?
かわいい	ですよ。	It sure is cute.

Whose is it?

Core

だれの	whose
わたしの	my
ぼくの	my (boys)
せんせいの	teacher's
エマ(えま)さんの	Emma's

Pet food

Core

えさ	pet food
やさい	vegetables
くさ	grass
さかな	fish
にく	meat
みず	water

Verbs

Core

たべます	eat
のみます	drink

I thought ducks said 'quack quack'!

In Japan, children are taught that the sound a duck makes is ガーガー(がーがー). Here are some other animal sounds that are usually written in *katakana*.

ワンワン(わんわん)	dogs
ニャーニャー(にゃーにゃー)	cats
モーモー(もーもー)	cows
メーメー(めーめー)	sheep
ブーブー(ぶーぶー)	pigs

05

八十九

ISBN 9780170196826

ワンワン、ガーガー

ももたろう

むかし　むかし、　おじいさんと　おばあさんが すんで　いました。Once upon a time, there lived an old man and an old woman. Every day, the old man went into the mountains to collect firewood, and the old woman washed their clothes in the river. One day, as the woman was washing the clothes, she saw a huge peach bobbing downstream.

どんぶりこっこ、 どんぶりこ

なんとも、　おいしそうな　もも!

She struggled to drag it out of the water and then carefully carried it home, where she waited to show it to her husband. When her husband saw it, he too was shocked. It looked so delicious, they could not wait to cut it.

When they sliced it in half, to their amazement, out popped a healthy, chubby baby boy. They were delighted with the child and they called him ももたろう (peach boy). The boy always ate his dinner and so grew up big and strong.

One day, the boy said, 「おにがしまに　おにたいじに いきます。」 'I am going to Ogre Island to get rid of the ogres.' The ogres had been harassing the villagers for years. The old man and the old woman tried to talk him out of it, but he was determined.

05

九
十
90

ワンワン、ガーガー

ISBN 9780170196826

The day came for the boy to leave. The old woman made him the best きびだんご (dumplings) in all of Japan to eat on the way. He packed the きびだんご and put on his はれぎ (best clothes), and he set off.

After a while he met an いぬ (dog).

「ももたろうさん、　ももたろうさん、　どこ いくの?」 'Momotaro-san, where are you going?' asked the dog.

「おにがしまへ　おにたいじに　いく。」 'I am going to Ogre Island to get rid of the ogres,' he replied.

「日本一の　きびだんごを　一つ　ください。 おとも　します。」 'If you give me one of Japan's best きびだんご, I will come with you,' said the dog.

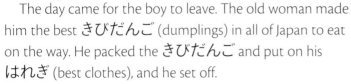

おにがしまへ
おにたいじに　いきます。

日本一の　きびだんごを　一つ　ください。
おとも　します。

The boy gave the dog a きびだんご, and they travelled on together. A little further along they met a さる (monkey).

「ももたろうさん、　ももたろうさん、　どこ いくの?」 'Momotaro-san, where are you going?' asked the monkey. 「おにがしまへ　おにたいじに　いく。」 'I am going to Ogre Island to get rid of the ogres,' he replied.

「日本一の　きびだんごを　一つ　ください。 おとも　します。」 'If you give me one of Japan's best きびだんご, I will come with you,' said the monkey.

The boy gave the monkey a きびだんご, and the three travelled on together. A little further along, they met a きじ (pheasant).

「ももたろうさん、　ももたろうさん、　どこ いくの?」 'Momotaro-san, where are you going?' asked the pheasant.

「おにがしまへ　おにたいじに　いく。」 'I am going to Ogre Island to get rid of the ogres,' he replied.

「日本一の　きびだんごを　一つ　ください。 おとも　します。」 'If you give me one of Japan's best きびだんご, I will come with you,' said the pheasant.

Eventually the boy, the dog, the monkey and the pheasant reached the sea, where they boarded a boat and headed for おにがしま (Ogre Island).

05

九
十
一

91

ISBN 9780170196826

ワンワン、ガーガー

When they arrived at the island, they found their way blocked by a big, black gate. The monkey climbed over the gate and unlocked it from the other side, and the pheasant flew over the island to find the ogres. They found the ogres drunk and partying in the middle of the island.

「ぼくは　日本一（にほんいち）の　ももたろう！　おにどもを　せいばつに　きた！」 'I am the great Momotaro! I have come to punish you for harassing the people of my village,' said Momotaro.

The dog bit the ogres, the monkey scratched them, the pheasant pecked out their eyes, and Momotaro slashed them with his sword.

「ごめんなさい、　もう　しません！」 Defeated, the ogres cried, 'We are so sorry! We will not do it again!'

Momotaro had fulfilled his dream of defeating the ogres. Momotaro and his friends took back all of the stolen treasure and headed for home.

めでたし、　めでたし。 And they all lived happily ever after.

おしまい。 The end.

Have a think

1 Three animals accompany Momotaro on this quest to defeat the ogres. Why do you think those particular animals appear in the story?
2 Certain expressions are used in folktales in English and Japanese. Can you identify any of these Japanese expressions in the story?
3 What is the moral of this folktale? What do stories like this tell us about people?
4 What other stories or folktales do you know that talk about heroes? What are the similarities between Japanese folktales and other folktales you know?

Have a go

1 Act out the story of Momotaro with English narration and Japanese dialogue.
2 If you like this story, read some other Japanese folktales. Go to Kids Web Japan and read some more.

05

九十二

92

ワンワン、ガーガー

ISBN 9780170196826

おかし

パクパクおりがみ

Let's make a パクパクおりがみ (chatterbox) to chatter with the Japanese words you have learnt so far. Ask your teacher how! Have fun!

うたいましょう

♪ The animal song

Sing along to the tune of the Japanese children's song「こぶた、　たぬき、　きつね、　ねこ」.
Sing the words on the left. Then, do the actions as you sing the animal noise.
Finally, put them both together!

あひる（ガーガー）	(Shape your hands like a beak in front of your mouth.)
きんぎょ（スイスイ）	(Swish your hands like a fin.)
いぬ（ワンワン）	(Make your hands into dog's ears.)
ねこ（ニャオ）	(Make cat's whiskers with your fingers.)
うま（ヒヒヒーン）	(Hold the reins and gallop.)
うさぎ（ピョンピョン）	(Put your two hands up in front of you, then bounce, bounce.)
とり（ピピピ）	(Wave your arms and 'fly'.)
へび（ニョロニョロ）	(Shape your hands like a snake's head.)

Ioan-Liviu Orletchi

♪ The pet food song

Sing this to the tune of 'Jingle Bells'.

えさ、　えさ、　えさ、
えさ、　えさ、　えさ、
くさ、　くさ、　くさ、　くさ、　さかな!
にく、にく、にく、にく、にく、にく、にく、にく
みず、　みず、　みず、　やさい!

えさ、　えさ、　えさ、
えさ、　えさ、　えさ、
くさ、　くさ、　くさ、　くさ、　さかな!
にく、にく、にく、にく、にく、にく、にく、にく
みず、　みず、　みず、　やさい!

ISBN 9780170196826

05

九十三

93

ワンワン、ガーガー

5.9

Here are some useful expressions from いただきます。

きょうは ペットの はなしを しましょう。
Let's talk about pets today.

いい です。
That's good.
That's okay.

そして
and

なまえは なん ですか。
What is its name?

うそー！
You're kidding!

おもしろい ですね。
That's interesting, isn't it?

ひどーい！
That's disgusting!

おめでとう! Look at all of the things you have learnt in this unit! Go to your workbook and fill in the checklist at the end of the unit.

ワンワン、ガーガー

ISBN 9780170196826

パスタがすき！

メニュー

いただきます　96–8

Learn to:
- read a *manga* about eating and drinking
- understand a conversation

どんなあじ？　99–101

Learn to:
- ask about meals and respond
- ask about likes and dislikes and respond
- express likes and dislikes

つくりましょう！　102–3

Text types:
- recipe

べんきょうのベン　104–5

Learn to:
- read the *katakana* characters キ, コ, サ, シ, ソ, タ, チ, ヒ, ミ, ン, ジ, パ 、 ン and ピ
- read the words and expressions you will learn in this unit

ごはんとおかず　106–7

Learn about:
- food and drinks
- meals
- likes and dislikes
- verbs

テーブルマナー　108–9

Learn about:
- Japanese food

おはし　110

Learn about:
- writing and saying *katakana* words

おかし　111

Learn to:
- sing songs and perform a rap to help you remember new words

おしょうゆ　112

Learn about:
- other words that will make your Japanese sound natural

パスタがすき！

ISBN 9780170196826

Have a think

1 What famous landmark can you see from Hakone?
2 What do Kate and Yuusuke swap for lunch?
3 What do you notice about Harjono's lunch, compared with your lunch?
4 What does Harjono offer Yuki?
5 What does Harjono offer Takako?
6 Harjono offers Emma three things. What are they and which one does she like?
7 What was left for Harjono to eat?

ISBN 9780170196826

どんなあじ?

Asking about meals and responding

あさごはんに
なにを
たべますか。

と ー す と
トーストを
たべます。

なにを
のみますか。

お れ ん じ じ ゅ ー す
オレンジジュースを
のみます。

ひるごはんに　なにを
たべますか。

ぼくは　おべんとうと
け ー き
ケーキを　たべます。

ばんごはんに
なにを
たべますか。

わたしは　にくと
やさいを　たべます。
おちゃを　のみます。

ロールプレー

A	あさごはんに ひるごはんに ばんごはんに	なにを　たべますか。 なにを　のみますか。	
B	☐を ☐と　☐を	たべます。 のみます。	☐さんは？ ☐くんは？
A	わたしは ぼくは	☐を ☐と☐を	たべます。 のみます。

ISBN 9780170196826

パスタがすき！

Talking about likes and dislikes

Asking about likes and dislikes and responding

パスタがすき！

ISBN 9780170196826

Expressing likes and dislikes

The せつめい pages at the back of this book will give you even more information to help you talk about likes and dislikes, and meals. Just turn to page 225.

ロールプレー

A	___ が すき ですか。		
B	はい、	すき です。 だいすき です。	___さんは? ___くんは?
A	いいえ、	あんまり... きらい です。 だいきらい です。	
B	わたしは ぼくは	___が ___ です。	

06

百
一

101

パスタがすき!

つくりましょう!

Recipe

おこのみやきを　つくりましょう! Let's make *okonomiyaki*!
おこのみやき is a Japanese-style savoury pancake that is easy to make –
and even easier to eat!

おこのみ means 'as you like it', and やき means 'grilled'.

As it is such a popular dish in Japan, there are many recipes for
おこのみやき. Here is one of the easiest. Read the recipe with your teacher.

ざいりょう (Ingredients)

こむぎこ (plain flour) .... ½ cup (100 g)

たまご (eggs) 1

みず (water) .... ½ cup

キャベツ (shredded cabbage) .... 1 cup

ねぎ (sliced shallots/spring onions)........ ½ cup

にく (meat) .... 4 thin strips

えび (uncooked prawns) .... 4–6 (optional)

おこのみに　おおじて　ふりかけて　ください。
(Sprinkle on according to taste.)

- あおのり (seaweed flakes)
- かつおぶし (bonito flakes)
- おこのみやきソース
  (okonomiyaki sauce)
- マヨネーズ
  (mayonnaise, optional)

Useful words

いれます	put in
はしで	with chopsticks
フライパンで	in a frying pan
まぜます	stir
やきます	fry
のせます	put on top
ひっくりかえします	flip over

ISBN 9780170196826

つくりかた (Method)

1　たまごと　こむぎこと　みずを　いれます。　はしで　まぜます。

2　キャベツと　ねぎを　いれます。

3　フライパンで　やきます。

4　にくと　えびを　のせます。

5　ひっくりかえします。

6　ソースと　マヨネーズと　かつおぶしと　あおのりを　のせます。

できあがり。ひるごはんに　おこのみやきを　たべます。　いただきます!

Have a think

1　Read the recipe with your teacher.
2　What do you notice about all of the verbs?
3　Look at the language patterns. How would you say the following?
   - Put in some meat.
   - Put in some cheese.
   - Put in some vegetables.

Have a go

1　Cook おこのみやき and eat it!
2　Make a poster explaining おこのみやき.
3　Create an おこのみやき banner for your classroom.
4　Using this recipe as a model, write the recipe, including illustrations, for another Japanese dish.
5　Learn more about おこのみやき.
   - There are other styles of おこのみやき? Find one and describe it to the class.
   - What other recipes can you find for おこのみやき?
   - When did おこのみやき become popular in Japan?

06

百
三

ISBN 9780170196826

パスタがすき!

カタカナ

  6.3

Use the chart to say the *katakana* sounds. Your teacher will help you.

*	w	r	y	m	h	n	t	s	k	
ン n	ワ	ラ	ヤ	マ	ハ	ナ	タ	サ	カ	ア a
		リ		ミ	ヒ	ニ	チ chi	シ shi	キ	イ i
		ル	ユ	ム	フ fu	ヌ	ツ tsu	ス	ク	ウ u
		レ		メ	ヘ	ネ	テ	セ	ケ	エ e
	ヲ	ロ	ヨ	モ	ホ	ノ	ト	ソ	コ	オ o

Here are the *katakana* introduced in this unit.

ダ ta ソ so シ shi サ sa コ ko キ ki

ピ pi パ pa ジ ji ン n ミ mi ヒ hi チ chi

Can you figure out these ice-cream flavours using the *katakana* you know?

チョコレート　　ストロベリー

チョコレートミント　　ラムレーズン

チョコチーズケーキ　　バニラ

パスタがすき！

ISBN 9780170196826

Then, use the look, think and count method to see if you can read these words.

コーンフレーク　　トースト　　サンドイッチ　　サラダ

パン　ピザ　チキン　パスタ　ソーセージ

ハンバーガー　カレーライス　チーズ　アイスクリーム

ケーキ　ミルク　オレンジジュース　コーヒー　コーラ

Look at the signs. Do you notice how *katakana* is used to write English words? Try to find each of the *katakana* in your *katakana* chart.

6.1, 6.4

ISBN 9780170196826

パスタがすき！

06

百
五

105

ごはんとおかず

ごはん

Asking about meals and responding

あさごはんに ひるごはんに ばんごはんに	なにを　たべますか。
For breakfast, For lunch, For dinner,	what do you eat?
トーストを ごはんと　おかずを おちゃを	たべます。 のみます。
Toast Rice and side dishes Green tea	I eat I drink

MILKY SHAVED ICE
完熟フルーツのミルクかき氷
厳選したすりつぶし果実のフルーツピューレが素材を感じる舌触り。

パッションミルク 390円
バナナミルク 390円
マンゴーミルク 390円
ラズベリーミルク 390円
ピーチミルク 390円
レッドベリーミルク 390円

Magdy Habib, Cameron Stevens and Christopher Kocx

Talking about likes and dislikes

Asking about likes and dislikes and responding

すしが　すき　ですか。 カレーライスが　すき　ですか。	
Do you like sushi? Do you like curry and rice?	
はい、　だいすき　です。 はい、　すき　です。 いいえ、　あんまり… いいえ、　きらい　です。 いいえ、　だいきらい　です。	
Yes, I love it. Yes, I like it. No, not really. No, I do not like it. No, I hate it.	

Expressing likes and dislikes

わたしは ぼくは せんせいは	すしが　だいすき　です。 サラダが　すき　です。 ピザが　きらい　です。 にくが　だいきらい　です。
I I The teacher	love/loves sushi. like/likes salad. do/does not like pizza. hate/hates meat.

パスタがすき！

ISBN 9780170196826

おかず

Food

コーンフレーク	cornflakes
トースト	toast
たまご	eggs
パン	bread
サンドイッチ	sandwich
ハンバーガー	hamburger
ごはん	rice
ピザ	pizza
チキン	chicken
パスタ	pasta
ソーセージ	sausage
サラダ	salad
さかな	fish
カレーライス	curry rice
にく	meat
やさい	vegetables
チーズ	cheese
くだもの	fruit
おかし	sweets
アイスクリーム	ice-cream
チョコレート	chocolate
ケーキ	cake
おこのみやき	okonomiyaki

Drinks

Core

ミルク	milk
オレンジジュース	orange juice
おちゃ	green tea
こうちゃ	English (black) tea
コーヒー	coffee
コーラ	cola

Meals

Core

あさごはん	breakfast
ひるごはん	lunch
ばんごはん	dinner

Likes and dislikes

Core

だいすき	love
すき	like
あんまり…	not really
きらい	do not like
だいきらい	hate

Verbs

Core

たべます	eat
のみます	drink
たべません	do not eat
のみません	do not drink

Joining words

Core

そして	and
でも	but

06

ISBN 9780170196826 パスタがすき！

わしょく（日本のたべもの）

What is typical Japanese food? Well, there are many different types of Japanese food and they are all typical.

Unlike some countries where all kinds of food are available at the one restaurant, Japan has sushi restaurants for sushi, yakitori restaurants for yakitori and udon restaurants for udon.

すし
てんぷら
さしみ
やきそば
やきとり
みそしる
うどん
コロッケ
きつねそば
うなぎ
おせちりょうり
しゃぶしゃぶ

Photos by Alamy, Getty Images, Robert Simons, Shutterstock.com, Corbis/Amanaimages, Magdy Habib, Cameron Stevens and Christopher Kocx

06

パスタがすき！

ISBN 9780170196826

すきやき

おこのみやき

おべんとう

ケーキ

あんみつと まっちゃ

くだもの

わがし（日本のおかし）

ぱふぇ
パフェ

Have a think

1 Of the dishes pictured, which do you think are for special occasions? Which are everyday foods?
2 Which dishes do you think would normally be eaten at lunchtime?
3 Of the Japanese dishes pictured, which do you think are well known in Australia?
4 Why do you think sushi has become so popular as a take-away food in Australia?
5 What other popular dishes in Australia have been introduced from other cultures?
6 As a class, find out what some of your classmates' favourite dishes are. How many of the favourite dishes come from other cultures?

Have a go

6.2, 6.5

1 Check out your local supermarket for Japanese ingredients. List the Japanese foods you find.
2 With a group of friends, do some research to find a Japanese recipe that you can try to make. Then, make a *MasterChef*–style video to show your class.
3 Interview your grandparents, parents, brothers and sisters about their favourite foods. Ask older family members about foods that were popular when they were young. Make a timeline of popular foods in Australia across the generations. What factors could have influenced your findings?

06

百
九
....
109

Writing and saying katakana words

When *katakana* words are borrowed from other languages, their pronunciation usually changes. Some sounds used in English and other languages, such as 'v' or 'th', do not exist in Japanese. To say words or names containing those sounds, Japanese people must modify the pronunciation.

The following words all came to Japanese from English. How much of a change in pronunciation do you hear?

- ペン   pen
- チョコレート   chocolate
- コンピューター   computer
- クリスマス   Christmas
- クール   cool

- タクシー   taxi
- ハンバーガー   hamburger
- ビデオ   video
- ネイサン   Nathan
- マシュー   Matthew

Long sounds

In *katakana*, long sounds are written with a dash ー, called ぼう. Can you pick out which sounds are made longer by ー?

- ケーキ   cake
- スケート   skate

- アイスクリーム   ice-cream
- ハンバーガー   hamburger

When you are writing *katakana* long sounds, you have to be careful. The character will change depending on whether you are writing horizontally (left to right) or vertically (top to bottom).

ケーキ

スケート

アイスクリーム

ハンバーガー

あまり or あんまり?

あまり and あんまり both mean the same thing: 'not much' or 'not really'. The only difference is ん, which shows emphasis and polite hesitation.

Usually, あんまり is used in conversation, and あまり is used in writing. When you want to put more emphasis on the 'not much' part during a conversation, use あんまり.

Magdy Habib, Cameron Stevens and Christopher Kocx

パスタがすき！   ISBN 9780170196826

おかし

うたいましょう

やきとり

♪ おいしいごはん

Sing this song to the tune of 'Frère Jacques'.

あさごはん、　あさごはん
おいしい、　おいしい
たまごと　パン、　たまごと　パン
だいすき、　だいすき

ひるごはん、　ひるごはん
おいしい、　おいしい、
おちゃと　おべんとう、　おちゃと　おべんとう
だいすき、　だいすき

ばんごはん、　ばんごはん
おいしい、　おいしい
サラダと　チキン、　サラダと　チキン
だいすき、　だいすき

おべんとう

♪ Sakana, sakana

Sing this song to the tune of 'Sakura, Sakura'.
Can you recognise each of the Japanese foods
in the song?

さかな、　さかな
やきとり、　てんぷら
みそしる、　さしみ
ごはんと　うめぼし
おちゃ、　すし、　おにぎり
わさび、　わさび
おこのみやき

おかず

06

ISBN 9780170196826

パスタがすき！

おしょうゆ

Here are some useful expressions from いただきます。

ひるやすみ です。
It is lunchtime.

おべんとうを たべて ください。
Please eat your packed lunch.

おいしそう!
It looks delicious!
おいしい!
Delicious!
うーん、 おいしい です。
Mmm, it is delicious.

じゃあ、 どうぞ。
Well then, here it is.

まいにち
every day

ぼくも / わたしも
I/me too

おめでとう! Look at all of the things you have learnt in this unit! Go to your workbook and fill in the checklist at the end of the unit.

Shutterstock.com

パスタが すき!

ISBN 9780170196826

いつですか

メニュー

いただきます　114–16

Learn to:
- read a *manga* about calendars and dates
- understand a conversation

どんなあじ？　117–19

Learn to:
- ask the day and respond
- ask the date and respond
- ask when an event will take place and respond

つくりましょう！　120–1

Text types:
- calendar

べんきょうのベン　122–4

Learn to:
- read the *kanji* characters 日, 月, 火, 水, 木, 金, 土, 曜, 休
- understand how *kanji* can be combined
- read the *katakana* characters ク, テ, マ, ヤ and レ
- read the words and expressions you will learn in this unit

ごはんとおかず　125–7

Learn about:
- days
- dates
- months
- events
- time words

テーブルマナー　128–31

Learn about:
- festivals and celebrations in Japan

おかし　132

Learn to:
- sing songs to help you remember new words

おしょうゆ　133

Learn about:
- other words that will make your Japanese sound natural

いただきます

Find extra vocabulary on p. 133

いつですか

ISBN 9780170196826

テスト？　えええ！

なん曜^{よう}日^び　ですか。

ひぇええ！　やだー！

月曜^{げつよう}日^び　です。

はい、いい　ですか。
きいて　ください。
五月^{ごがつ}　九日^{ここのか}は
テスト^{てすと}　です。

しずかに！　しずかに！
五月^{ごがつ}　九日^{ここのか}、テスト^{てすと}。
かいて　ください。

③

はーい！

五月^{ごがつ}　十八日^{じゅうはちにち}は
えんそく　です。

五月^{ごがつ}　十八日^{じゅうはちにち}、水曜日^{すいようび}、
えんそく。　かいて
　　　　　ください。

わーい！　えんそく
　　だいすき！

パチパチ
キャー！

5月18日

五月^{ごがつ}　十八日^{じゅうはちにち}、
えんそく。
はい。

5月18日
えん

④

十九日^{じゅうくにち}、　二十日^{はつか}、
二十一日^{にじゅういちにち}は　がっこうの
キャンプ^{きゃんぷ}　です。　みなさん、
かいて　ください。　がっこうの
キャンプ^{きゃんぷ}は　十九日^{じゅうくにち}、
二十日^{はつか}、　二十一日^{にじゅういちにち}
です。　できましたか。

えっー!!
シャワーは??

CAMP

⑤

ISBN 9780170196826

1 What are the dates of the Golden Week holidays?
2 Japan has many public holidays. How does this compare with the public holidays in your country?
3 What is the date of the test? What day of the week is it?
4 What is the date of the excursion? What day of the week is it?
5 What is the date of the school camp? What day of the week is it?
6 When is Emma's birthday party?
7 What is happening on 31 May?

ISBN 9780170196826

どんなあじ？

Asking the day and responding

きょうは　なん曜日（ようび）ですか。

土曜日（どようび）です。

きょうは　なん曜日（ようび）ですか。

きょうは　木曜日（もくようび）です。

パーティー（ぱーてぃー）は　なん曜日（ようび）ですか。

金曜日（きんようび）です。

ロールプレー

A	きょうは □は	なん曜日（ようび）ですか。
B	きょうは □は	□曜日（ようび）です。

ISBN 9780170196826

いつですか

07

Asking the date and responding

きょうは　なん月　なん日　ですか。

六月　十二日　です。

えんそくは　なん月　なん日　ですか。

九月　十九日　です。

たかこさんの　たんじょうびは
なん月　なん日　ですか。

十二月　二十三日　です。

ロールプレー

A	きょうは □□は	なん月　なん日　ですか。
B	きょうは □□は	□月　□日　です。

いつですか

ISBN 9780170196826

Asking when an event will take place and responding

ばーてぃー
パーティーは　いつ　ですか。

に　がつ　にじゅうはちにち
二月　二十八日　です。

うんどうかいは　いつ　ですか。

ど　よう　び
土曜日　です。

ゆうすけくんの
たんじょうびは
いつ　ですか。

あした　です。

> The せつめい pages at the back of
> this book will give you even more
> information to help you talk about
> days, dates, months and when events
> happen. Just turn to page 226.

ロールプレー

A	ばーてぃー パーティーは □は	いつ　ですか。
B	ばーてぃー パーティーは □は	がつ　　　にち □月　□日　です。 ようび □曜日　です。 □　です。

つくりましょう！

7.2 Calendar

The Japanese calendar follows the Western calendar, which was introduced into Japan in the late nineteenth century. Before then, the Chinese calendar was used.

In Japanese, the days of the week are named after the sun and the moon, and the five elements of gold, wood, water, fire and earth.

四月

日曜日	月曜日	火曜日	水曜日	木曜日	金曜日	土曜日
					一日 すいえい たいかい	二日
三日	四日	五日	六日	七日	八日	九日
十日	十一日 きゃんぷ キャンプ	十二日 きゃんぷ キャンプ	十三日	十四日	十五日 いーすたー イースター の やす 休み	十六日 いーすたー イースター の やす 休み
十七日 いーすたー イースター の やす 休み	十八日 いーすたー イースター の やす 休み	十九日	二十日	二十一日	二十二日 ともだちの たんじょうび	二十三日
二十四日	二十五日 アンザック デー	二十六日	二十七日	二十八日	二十九日 しょうわの日	三十日

しがつ　じゅうごにち　しがつ　じゅうはちにち　　いーすたー　　やす
四月　十五日〜四月　十八日は　イースターの　休み　です。

それから、　すいえいたいかいは　四月　一日　です。
　　　　　　　　　　　　　　　　　　しがつ　ついたち
きゃんぷ　　　しがつ　じゅういちにち　じゅうににち
キャンプは　四月　十一日と　十二日　です。

ともだちの　たんじょうびは　四月　二十二日　です。
　　　　　　　　　　　　　　　しがつ　にじゅうににち
ぱーてぃー　　　　　　ごがつ　じゅうよっか
パーティーは　五月　十四日　です。

えんそくは　五月　十七日　です。
　　　　　　ごがつ　じゅうしちにち
ひらがなの　テストは　五月　二十六日　です。
　　　　　てすと　　　ごがつ　にじゅうろくにち
うんどうかいは　五月　三十一日　です。
　　　　　　　　ごがつ　さんじゅういちにち

ISBN 9780170196826

五月

日曜日	月曜日	火曜日	水曜日	木曜日	金曜日	土曜日
一日	二日	三日 けんぽう きねん日	四日 みどりの日	五日 こどもの日	六日	七日
八日 ははの日	九日	十日	十一日	十二日	十三日	十四日 パーティー！
十五日	十六日	十七日 えんそく	十八日	十九日	二十日	二十一日
二十二日	二十三日	二十四日 エマさんの たんじょうび	二十五日	二十六日 ひらがなの テスト	二十七日	二十八日
二十九日	三十日	三十一日 うんどうかい				

ゴールデン　ウィーク
四月　二十九日は　しょうわの日　です。　休み　です。
四月　三十日は　土曜日　です。　休み　です。
五月　一日は　日曜日　です。　休み　です。
五月　三日は　けんぽうきねん日　です。　休み　です。
五月　四日は　みどりの日　です。　休み　です。
五月　五日は　こどもの日　です。　休み　です。
四月　二十九日〜五月　五日は　ゴールデン　ウィーク　です。　やったー！

Useful words

しょうわの日	Showa Emperor's Birthday
けんぽうきねん日	Constitution Day
みどりの日	Greenery Day
こどもの日	Children's Day
ははの日	Mothers' Day

Have a go

1　Create a calendar for a month in Japan and another, also in Japanese, for the same month in Australia. Write in as many events and holidays as you can in each calendar. Then, write short sentences in Japanese saying when each event takes place.

ISBN 9780170196826

いつですか

かんじ

Each of the *kanji* used to write the days of the week originated from pictures of nature or the elements.

日	月	火	水	木
sun, daylight, day	moon, month	fire	water	tree

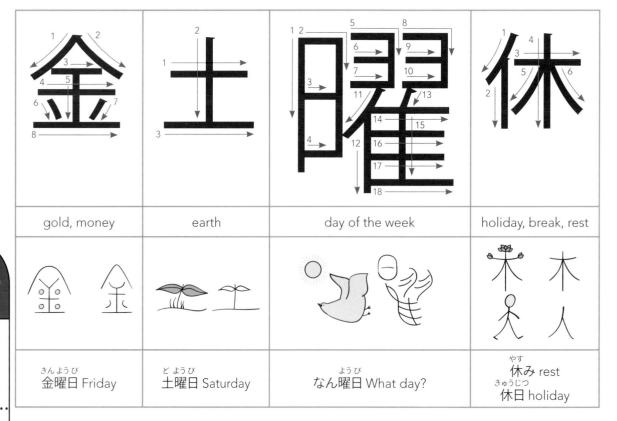

| 日曜日 Sunday
（にちようび）
クリスマスの日（ひ）
Christmas Day | 一月 January（いちがつ）
月曜日 Monday（げつようび） | 火曜日 Tuesday（かようび） | 水 water（みず）
水曜日 Wednesday（すいようび） | 木曜日 Thursday（もくようび） |

金	土	曜	休
gold, money	earth	day of the week	holiday, break, rest

| 金曜日 Friday（きんようび） | 土曜日 Saturday（どようび） | なん曜日 What day?（ようび） | 休み rest（やす）
休日 holiday（きゅうじつ） |

ISBN 9780170196826

Kanji are very logical and can be combined to build meaning. However, sometimes the pronunciation or 'reading' of the character changes. For example, 日 can be read in four different ways, but it will always mean 'sun' or 'day'.

- 日曜日 ⟨にちようび⟩ Sunday
- 月曜日 ⟨げつようび⟩ Monday
- クリスマスの日 ⟨くりすますのひ⟩ Christmas Day
- 三日 ⟨みっか⟩ 3rd

To write the days of the week, add the characters 曜日 ⟨ようび⟩ to the day of the week character.

- 水曜日 ⟨すいようび⟩ Wednesday

To write the months of the year, add the character 月 ⟨がつ⟩ to the number of the month.

- 五月 ⟨ごがつ⟩ May (the fifth month)

To write dates, add the character 日 ⟨にち⟩ to the number of the date.

- 十六日 ⟨じゅうろくにち⟩ 16th

You can put them all together to write the date.

- 五月十六日（水曜日）⟨ごがつ じゅうろくにち すいようび⟩ Wednesday 16 May

Each day, try writing the date in Japanese at the top of your work.

Did you know that the first day of each month, 一日 ⟨ついたち⟩, has a special reading? It was originally written as 月立 ⟨ついたち⟩ by combining the characters for 'moon' and 'standing'. On the first day of the month the moon looks as though it is standing because it is narrow and vertical.

See if you can read these.

三十一日	水曜日	二十九日	五日	十二日
九月	十月	土曜日	木曜日	十六日	二十八日
四日	火曜日	三日	一日	日曜日	二日	四月
月曜日	十二月	十七日	七月	金曜日	五月

百二十三

ISBN 9780170196826

いつですか

カタカナ

Use the chart to say the *katakana* sounds.
Your teacher will help you.

*	w	r	y	m	h	n	t	s	k		
ン n	ワ	ラ	ヤ	マ	ハ	ナ	タ	サ	カ	ア	a
		リ		ミ	ヒ	ニ	チ chi	シ shi	キ	イ	i
		ル	ユ	ム	フ fu	ヌ	ツ tsu	ス	ク	ウ	u
		レ		メ	ヘ	ネ	テ	セ	ケ	エ	e
	ヲ	ロ	ヨ	モ	ホ	ノ	ト	ソ	コ	オ	o

Here are the *katakana* introduced in this unit.

レ re　　ヤ ya　　マ ma　　テ te　　ク ku

Then, use the look, think and count method to see if you can read these words.

キャンプ　　ゴールデン　ウィーク　　テスト

クリスマス　　パーティー　　カレンダー

ISBN 9780170196826

ごはんとおかず

1.3

ごはん

> Did you notice how you can say
> パーティーは　金曜日　です
> (the party is on Friday) and also
> 金曜日は　パーティー　です
> (Friday is the party)?

Asking the day and responding

きょうは パーティーは	なん曜日　ですか。
Today The party	what day is it?
きょうは パーティーは	土曜日　です。
Today The party	is Saturday.

Asking the date and responding

きょうは えんそくは	なん月　なん日　ですか。
Today The excursion	what date is it?
きょうは えんそくは	六月　十二日　です。 十五日　です。
Today The excursion	is 12 June. is the 15th.

Asking when an event will take place and responding

パーティーは ゆうすけくんの　たんじょうびは	いつ　ですか。
The party, Yuusuke's birthday,	when is it?
パーティーは ゆうすけくんの　たんじょうびは	十一月　十二日　です。 金曜日　です。 あした　です。
The party Yuusuke's birthday	is 12 November. is Friday. is tomorrow.

07

百二十五

125

ISBN 9780170196826

いつですか

おかず

Events

Core

キャンプ (きゃんぷ)	camp
パーティー (ぱーてぃー)	party
テスト (てすと)	test
えんそく	excursion
休み (やす)	holiday
たんじょうび	birthday
ダンスパーティー (だんすぱーてぃー)	dance party
うんどうかい	sports carnival
すいえいたいかい	swimming carnival

Days

Core

なん曜日 (ようび)	What day?
日曜日 (にちようび)	Sunday
月曜日 (げつようび)	Monday
火曜日 (かようび)	Tuesday
水曜日 (すいようび)	Wednesday
木曜日 (もくようび)	Thursday
金曜日 (きんようび)	Friday
土曜日 (どようび)	Saturday

Time words

Core

いつ	when
きょう	today
あした	tomorrow

Months

Core

なん月 (がつ)	What month?
一月 (いちがつ)	January
二月 (にがつ)	February
三月 (さんがつ)	March
四月 (しがつ)	April
五月 (ごがつ)	May
六月 (ろくがつ)	June
七月 (しちがつ)	July
八月 (はちがつ)	August
九月 (くがつ)	September
十月 (じゅうがつ)	October
十一月 (じゅういちがつ)	November
十二月 (じゅうにがつ)	December

いつですか

ISBN 9780170196826

Dates

なん日 (にち)	What date?	十六日 (じゅうろくにち)	16th
一日 (ついたち)	1st	十七日 (じゅうしちにち)	17th
二日 (ふつか)	2nd	十八日 (じゅうはちにち)	18th
三日 (みっか)	3rd	十九日 (じゅうくにち)	19th
四日 (よっか)	4th	二十日 (はつか)	20th
五日 (いつか)	5th	二十一日 (にじゅういちにち)	21st
六日 (むいか)	6th	二十二日 (にじゅうににち)	22nd
七日 (なのか)	7th	二十三日 (にじゅうさんにち)	23rd
八日 (ようか)	8th	二十四日 (にじゅうよっか)	24th
九日 (ここのか)	9th	二十五日 (にじゅうごにち)	25th
十日 (とおか)	10th	二十六日 (にじゅうろくにち)	26th
十一日 (じゅういちにち)	11th	二十七日 (にじゅうしちにち)	27th
十二日 (じゅうににち)	12th	二十八日 (にじゅうはちにち)	28th
十三日 (じゅうさんにち)	13th	二十九日 (にじゅうくにち)	29th
十四日 (じゅうよっか)	14th	三十日 (さんじゅうにち)	30th
十五日 (じゅうごにち)	15th	三十一日 (さんじゅういちにち)	31st

Alamy

Days of the week

Here are some memory-jogging sentences to help you remember the days of the week.

日 (にち) On a sunny Sunday, your dog has an **itch**, so you give it a wash.

月 (げつ) On Monday, everyone **gets** up in the morning and goes to school.

火 (か) On Tuesday, you go by **car** to school again!

水 (すい) On Wednesday, it is your **swi**mming day.

木 (もく) On Thursday, you **muck** around on your computer!

金 (きん) On Friday, you eat **kin**g fish and chips!

土 (ど) Saturday opens the **do**or to the weekend.

ISBN 9780170196826

07

百二十七

いつですか

テーブルマナー

日本の一ねん
にほん いち

Japan is a country of many まつり (festivals). Many are associated with the changes in the seasons and their effects on the weather and agriculture. Festivals are often celebrated in the grounds of the local shrine, and おみこし (portable shrines) are often carried around during a festival in the hope that the good spirits of local gods can be spread around the community.

せつぶん
二月三日

On 二月三日 (3 February) people throw roasted soya beans around the house to bring good fortune, saying おにはそと、 ふくはうち, which means 'devils out, good fortune in'. Some shrines also hold special bean-throwing ceremonies. Children especially like this festival.
にがつ みっか

おしょうがつ
一月一日～一月三日

ひなまつり
三月三日

おしょうがつ (New Year) in Japan is the most important celebration of the year. Japanese people often travel home to spend time with their families. On New Year's Day, they visit local shrines to pray for good health and happiness for the coming year. They send ねんがじょう (New Year's cards) to wish each other a happy New Year. New Year is also traditionally a time to eat おもち (rice cakes), which are made at the end of December by pounding hot rice in a wooden trough.

ひなまつり is the festival for girls in Japan. On this day, ひなにんぎょう (Hina dolls) and peach blossoms are displayed in homes where there are female children. Some girls have parties with special food such as ひしもち (diamond-shaped rice cakes), しろざけ (sweet rice wine) and あられ (rice crackers).

07

百
二
十
八

いつですか

ISBN 9780170196826

はなみ
四月

Shutterstock.com/Paul Atkinson

When the cherry blossoms bloom in April, people like to have picnics under the cherry trees. They listen to music, dance and play cards.

こどもの日
五月五日

こどもの日 (Children's Day) is a public holiday. It is a celebration for boys in the family. Ornamental samurai helmets and swords are displayed inside the houses of male children, and こいのぼり (carp kites) are flown on poles outside. Special festival food is eaten.

ゴールデン　ウィーク
四月二十九日〜五月五日

Getty Images

つゆ
六月

The rainy season in Japan is the time when it rains and rains and rains. Of course, the rain is welcomed by farmers as it is necessary for a good harvest.

7.4

たなばた
七月七日

Shutterstock.com

ゴールデン　ウィーク (Golden Week) is a special week made up of four public holidays:

• しょうわの日, Showa Emperor's Birthday (29 April)

• けんぽうきねん日, Constitution Day (3 May)

• みどりの日, Greenery Day (4 May)

• こどもの日, Children's Day (5 May).

People often take holidays during this time.

People decorate bamboo with streamers and other decorations for たなばた. They also write wishes on colourful paper and attach these to the bamboo. This festival originated from a Chinese legend about the stars in the summer sky.

07

百二十九

129

ISBN 9780170196826

いつですか

おぼん
八月十五日

あきまつり
九月

おぼん is a Buddhist festival that celebrates the return of the souls of one's ancestors. とうろう (lanterns) are lit to welcome the ancestors back to the house. All around Japan people celebrate with ぼんおどり (folk dancing) and はなび (fireworks).

あきまつり (Autumn Festival) is celebrated at different times in autumn in different parts of Japan. It is a festival for giving thanks to the gods for a good harvest. おみこし (portable shrines) are carried around the town by members of the community.

たいいくの日
十月

ぶんかの日
十一月三日

The second Monday in October is たいいくの日 (Sports Day) and is a public holiday throughout Japan. Around this time, many schools hold their annual うんどうかい (sports carnival).

On ぶんかの日 (Culture Day), the Emperor gives out awards for outstanding cultural contributions. Students are busy planning their own school's ぶんかさい (cultural festival), which is similar to a school open day or fête.

ISBN 9780170196826

七五三
十一月十五日

クリスマスの日
十二月二十五日

Merry Christmas
木苺のケーキ
¥550

しちごさん
七五三 is a festival held for five-year-old boys and three- and seven-year-old girls. In some parts of Japan, three-year-old boys also take part.

The traditional belief is that children of these ages are particularly prone to danger and bad luck. Parents dress their children in traditional きもの and visit local shrines to pray that their children will grow to be healthy and strong.

Although Christmas is a Christian celebration, and most Japanese people are not Christians, Christmas is now also celebrated in Japan. Christmas Day is not a public holiday in Japan, but department stores and shopping centres are beautifully decorated with Christmas decorations. Most houses have a Christmas tree and children are given Christmas presents.

Have a think ○○○○○○

1 How have the seasons in Japan influenced the way each Japanese festival is celebrated?
2 What factors influence how you celebrate festivals and yearly events?

Have a go ○○○○○○○○○○○○○○○

1 Research other Japanese festivals that are special to particular regions of Japan. Try to find out about any special food that is eaten, special clothes or costumes that are worn, activities that families do together on the day and the places people visit. What factors influence how the festival is celebrated?

07

百
三
十
一

131

いつですか

ISBN 9780170196826

Corbis/Michael S. Yamashita

おかし

うたいましょう

The days of the month song

Sing this song to the tune of 'Row, Row, Row Your Boat'.

ついたち、 ふつか、
みっか、 よっか、 いつか、
むいか、 なのか、 ようか、
ここのか、 とおか。

The days of the week song

Sing this song to the tune of 'Oh My Darling, Clementine' to remember the days of the week.

にちようび、
げつようび
か、 すい、 もく、 きん
どようび、
にちようび
Every day she/he makes us sing!

The festivals song

Sing this song to the tune of 'Bibbidi-Bobbidi-Boo'.

Verse 1
いちがつは　しょうがつで
ケーキを　たべましょう。
ケーキを、　ケーキを　たべましょう。
ケーキを　たべましょう。

Verse 2
にがつは　せつぶんで
ケーキを　たべましょう。
ケーキを、　ケーキを　たべましょう。
ケーキを　たべましょう。
(For the following verses, repeat the end of the verse above.)

Verse 3
さんがつは　ひなまつりで

Verse 4
しがつは　はなみで

Verse 5
ごがつは　こどものひで

Verse 6
ろくがつは　つゆで

Verse 7
しちがつは　たなばたで

Verse 8
はちがつは　おぼんで

Verse 9
くがつは　あきまつりで

Verse 10
じゅうがつは　うんどうかいで

Verse 11
じゅういちがつは　ぶんかさいで

Verse 12
じゅうにがつは　クリスマスで

いつですか

ISBN 9780170196826

おしょうゆ

Here are some useful expressions from いただきます.

やだー!
No!

えええ!
What?

いいね!
That's good!

やったー!
Yay!

わーい!
Wow!

うれしい!
I am so happy!

それから
and then

できましたか。
Have you done it yet?

なんの日 ですか。
What day is it?

ようすけ くん

メリー
クリスマス

メリー おめ

ことしも
よろしく
なぉみ より

すけじゅーる
スケジュール
schedule

かれんだー
カレンダー
calendar

そうだよ!
That's right! (informal boys' talk)
そうね!
That's right! (informal girls' talk)

おめでとう! Look at all of the things you have learnt in this unit! Go to your workbook and fill in the checklist at the end of the unit.

まるを して ください。
Please circle it.

がっこう
school

百
三
十
三

Unit 8

しゅみは？

メニュー

ISBN 9780170196826

しゅみは？

ISBN 9780170196826

Have a think

1 What is Tony's hobby?
2 What is Kenichi's hobby?
3 What sports can Kenichi play?
4 What sports does Yuusuke play?
5 What is Emma's hobby?
6 Look at the *manga* and identify the words used for sound effects.

7 Listen to the CD again and see if you can recognise how to say:
- What is your hobby?
- What kinds of sports do you play?
- Can you play sports?

しゅみは？

どんなあじ?

Asking about hobbies and interests and responding

しゅみは なん ですか。

からて です。

しゅみは なん ですか。

しゅみは ダンス です。

しゅみは なん ですか。

ぼくの しゅみは サーフィン です。

ロールプレー

A	しゅみは なん ですか。	
B	☐ です。 ☐ です。	☐さんは? ☐くんは?
A	わたしの ぼくの	しゅみは ☐ です。 しゅみは ☐ です。

Asking about sports and responding

どんな スポーツを しますか。

けんどうを します。

どんな スポーツを しますか。

わたしは すいえいを します。

どんな スポーツを しますか。

ぼくは やきゅうを します。

しゅみは?

ISBN 9780170196826

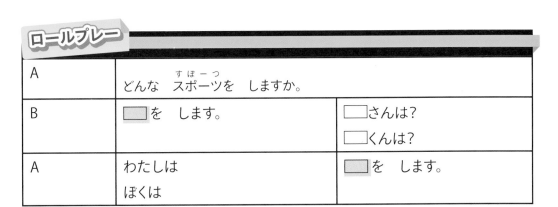

ロールプレー

A	どんな スポーツを しますか。	
B	◻ を します。	◻さんは? ◻くんは?
A	わたしは ぼくは	◻ を します。

Talking about what someone can do

Asking if someone can do something and responding

りょうりが できますか。

はい、 できます!

サーフィンが できますか。

はい、 すこし できます。

けんどうが できますか。

あんまり できません。

ギターが できますか。

いいえ、 できません。

ピアノが できますか。

ぜんぜん できません。

08

ISBN 9780170196826

Expressing what someone can do

じょうばが
できます。

りょうりが
すこし
できます。

わたしは
すいえいが
あんまり
できません。

ぼくは ゴルフが
できません。
ごるふ

せんせいは
スケートが
ぜんぜん
できません。
すけーと

The せつめい pages at the
back of this book will give
you even more information
to help you talk about
hobbies, interests and
sports, and other things
you are able to do. Just
turn to page 227.

ロールプレー

A	□が　できますか。		
	□が　できますか。		
B	はい、	できます。	□さんは？
		すこし　できます。	□くんは？
	いいえ、	できません。	
		あまり　できません。	
		ぜんぜん　できません。	
A	わたしは	□が	できます。
	ぼくは	□が	すこし　できます。
			できません。
			あまり　できません。
			ぜんぜん　できません。

しゅみは？

ISBN 9780170196826

カタカナ

Use the chart to say the *katakana* sounds. Your teacher will help you.

*	w	r	y	m	h	n	t	s	k	
ン n	ワ	ラ	ヤ	マ	ハ	ナ	タ	サ	カ	ア **a**
		リ		ミ	ヒ	ニ	チ chi	シ shi	キ	イ **i**
		ル	ユ	ム	フ fu	ヌ	ツ tsu	ス	ク	ウ **u**
		レ		メ	ヘ	ネ	テ	セ	ケ	エ **e**
	ヲ	ロ	ヨ	モ	ホ	ノ	ト	ソ	コ	オ **o**

Here are the *katakana* introduced in this unit.

ル ru　ホ ho　フ fu　ノ no　ネ ne　ツ tsu
ポ po　ボ bo　バ ba　ダ da　グ gu　ギ gi

Then, use the look, think and count method to see if you can read these words.

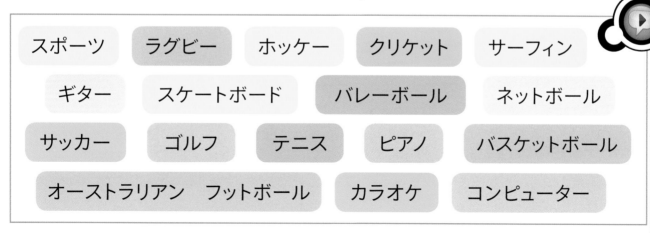

スポーツ　ラグビー　ホッケー　クリケット　サーフィン

ギター　スケートボード　バレーボール　ネットボール

サッカー　ゴルフ　テニス　ピアノ　バスケットボール

オーストラリアン　フットボール　カラオケ　コンピューター

ISBN 9780170196826

しゅみは？

08

百四十一

つくりましょう！

Interview

The new host of スター　チャット<ruby>スター<rt>すたー</rt></ruby>　<ruby>チャット<rt>ちゃっと</rt></ruby> is interviewing Justin Bieber, who is touring Japan. Bieber's Japanese fans are getting very excited and sending in questions that they would like the host to ask him. What questions would you want the host to ask? How will Bieber, with the help of his interpreter, answer? Here we go!

みなさん、　こんにちは。　きょうの　ゲスト<ruby>ゲスト<rt>げすと</rt></ruby>は　カナダ<ruby>カナダ<rt>かなだ</rt></ruby>の　スーパースター<ruby>スーパースター<rt>すーぱーすたー</rt></ruby>、　ジャスティン　ビーバー<ruby>ジャスティン<rt>じゃすてぃん</rt></ruby>　<ruby>ビーバー<rt>びーばー</rt></ruby>さん　です。　ジャスティン<ruby>ジャスティン<rt>じゃすてぃん</rt></ruby>さん、　こんにちは。　日本<ruby>日本<rt>にほん</rt></ruby>に　ようこそ。

- なんさい　ですか。
- たんじょうびは　いつ　ですか。
- カナダ<ruby>カナダ<rt>かなだ</rt></ruby>の　どこから　きましたか。
- いま、　どこに　すんで　いますか。

かぞくの　こと　ですが。

- なん<ruby>人<rt>にん</rt></ruby>　かぞく　ですか。
- おかあさんの　なまえは　なん　ですか。
- おとうとの　なまえは　なん　ですか。
- おとうとは　なんさい　ですか。
- ペット<ruby>ペット<rt>ぺっと</rt></ruby>が　いますか。

がっこうの　こと　ですが。

- がっこうの　なまえは　なんですか。
- がっこうが　すき　ですか。

Useful words

日本<ruby>日本<rt>にほん</rt></ruby>に　ようこそ	welcome to Japan
いま	now
かぞくの　こと　ですが	about your family ...
がっこうの　こと　ですが	about your school ...
しゅみの　こと　ですが	about your hobbies ...
さいごに	lastly
また、　日本<ruby>日本<rt>にほん</rt></ruby>に　きて　ください	please come to Japan again

しゅみは？

ISBN 9780170196826

つぎは、　<u>しゅみの　こと</u>　ですが。

- しゅみは　なん　ですか。
- どんな　おんがくが　すき　ですか。
- <ruby>ギター<rt>ぎたー</rt></ruby>が　できますか。
- どんな　<ruby>スポーツ<rt>すぽーつ</rt></ruby>を　します か。
- <ruby>日本<rt>にほん</rt></ruby>の　<ruby>スポーツ<rt>すぽーつ</rt></ruby>が　できますか。
- りょうりが　できますか。
- どんな　たべものが　すき　ですか。
- <ruby>日本<rt>にほん</rt></ruby>　りょうりが　すき　ですか。なにが　すき　ですか。
- ときどき　すしを　たべますか。

さいごに...
- <ruby>ガールフレンド<rt>がーるふれんど</rt></ruby>が　いますか。

<ruby>ジャスティン<rt>じゃすてぃん</rt></ruby>さん、　きょうは　どうも　ありがとう　ございました。

また　<ruby>日本<rt>にほん</rt></ruby>に　<u>きて　ください</u>。

Don't forget to use expressions like these!
ああ、　そう　ですか。
そう　ですねー。
おもしろい　ですね。
はい、　はい、　はい。

AAP Photo/Shuji Kajiyama

AAP Photo/Shuji Kajiyama

ISBN 9780170196826

しゅみは？

ごはんとおかず

ごはん

Asking about hobbies and interests and responding

しゅみは　なん　ですか。
What is your hobby?
からて　です。 しゅみは　ダンス　です。
It is karate. My hobby is dancing.

Asking about sports and responding

どんな　スポーツを　しますか。
What kind of sports do you play?
けんどうを　します。 わたしは　テニスを　します。
I do kendo. I play tennis.

Talking about what someone can do

Asking if someone can do something and responding

りょうりが フランスごが	できますか。
Cooking, French,	can you do it?
はい、	できます。 すこし　できます。
Yes,	I can. I can a little.
いいえ、	あまり　できません。 できません。 ぜんぜん　できません。
No,	I cannot do it very well. I cannot do it. I cannot do it at all.

Expressing what someone can do

わたしは ぼくは せんせいは	ホッケーが	できます。 すこし　できます。 あまり　できません。 できません。 ぜんぜん　できません。
I I The teacher		can do (play) hockey. can do (play) hockey a little. cannot do (play) hockey much. cannot do (play) hockey. cannot do (play) hockey at all.

Getty Images

08

百四十四

144

しゅみは？

ISBN 9780170196826

おかず

Hobbies and interests

Core

ピアノ (ぴあの)	piano
コンピューター (こんぴゅーたー)	computer
りょうり	cooking
おんがく	music
どくしょ	reading
ギター (ぎたー)	guitar
カラオケ (からおけ)	karaoke
ダンス (だんす)	dance

Languages

More

インドネシアご (いんどねしあご)	Indonesian
フランスご (ふらんす)	French
イタリアご (いたりあ)	Italian
えいご	English
ちゅうごくご	Chinese

Japanese traditional arts

More

いけばな	flower arrangement
さどう	tea ceremony
しょどう	calligraphy
からて	karate
あいきどう	aikido
きゅうどう	Japanese archery
じゅうどう	judo
けんどう	kendo

Can

Core

できます	I can do it
すこし　できます	I can do it a little
あまり　できません	I cannot do it very well
できません	I cannot do it
ぜんぜん　できません	I cannot do it at all

Sports

Core

スポーツ	sport
じょうば	horse-riding
サーフィン (さーふぃん)	surfing
バスケットボール (ばすけっとほーる)	basketball
ラグビー (らぐびー)	rugby
すいえい	swimming
ソフトボール (そふとほーる)	softball
クリケット (くりけっと)	cricket
ネットボール (ねっとほーる)	netball
オーストラリアン　フットボール (おーすとらりあん　ふっとほーる)	Australian rules football
バレーボール (ばれーほーる)	volleyball
ホッケー (ほっけー)	hockey
やきゅう	baseball
サッカー (さっかー)	soccer
ゴルフ (ごるふ)	golf
スキー (すきー)	skiing
スケート (すけーと)	skating
からて	karate
テニス (てにす)	tennis

しゅみは？

しゅみはなんですか

Japan has a rich history of traditional sports, arts and crafts.

The Japanese traditional arts often end with the character 道 <ruby>(どう)</ruby>, for example, 柔道 <ruby>(じゅうどう)</ruby> (judo), 空手道 <ruby>(からて どう)</ruby> (karate), 弓道 <ruby>(きゅうどう)</ruby> (Japanese archery), 合気道 <ruby>(あいきどう)</ruby> (aikido), いけばな or 華道 <ruby>(か どう)</ruby> (flower arranging) and 茶道 <ruby>(さ どう)</ruby> (tea ceremony).

The *kanji* 道 <ruby>(どう)</ruby> means 'passage', 'road' or 'way of life'. To truly master one of these traditional Japanese arts, both body and mind need to be trained, until the art virtually becomes a way of life.

けんどう
剣道

The kanji 剣 <ruby>(けん)</ruby> means 'sword' in English, so 剣道 <ruby>(けんどう)</ruby> is 'the way of the sword'. As the さむらい emerged during the eighth century in Japan, 剣術 <ruby>(けんじゅつ)</ruby> (the technique of using swords) also developed. During the relatively peaceful Edo Period of the early seventeenth century and until the eighteenth century, 剣術 <ruby>(けんじゅつ)</ruby> evolved into the current form of 剣道 <ruby>(けんどう)</ruby>.

In 剣道 <ruby>(けんどう)</ruby>, the technique of sword fighting and having a calm, humble and dedicated spirit are important. 「れいにはじまり、れいにおわる。」 (Begin with a bow, and end with a bow.)

In 剣道 <ruby>(けんどう)</ruby>, a しあい (match) takes about five minutes. The first player to score two points out of three is the winner. To obtain points, players need to hit their opponent in the めん (head), こて (forearm), どう (torso) or つき (throat).

ISBN 9780170196826

Getty Images

The *kanji* 弓 means 'bows and arrows'. As early as the fifteenth century, the use of bows and arrows as weapons developed into a martial art that disciplines the mind and body.

The modern form of 弓道 values manners and formality, and pursues a state of mind known as むしん, which values concentration and separating the mind from other thoughts.

The bows are made of laminated wood and bamboo and are just over 2 metres long. Archers shoot both short distances (28 metres) and long distances (60 metres).

きゅうどう
弓道

Getty Images

じゅうどう
柔道

Getty Images

じゅうどう
柔道 developed from the hand-to-hand combat martial art of じゅうじつ. In 1882, Kano Jigoro opened a now world-famous どうじょう (gymnasium) called こうどうかん and started teaching the present-day form of 柔道.

じゅうどう
柔道 is a form of self-defence that aims for both mental and physical strength. Players try to use their opponent's weight and strength to their own advantage. Throwing and gripping are the main techniques.

じゅうどう
柔道 became an official Olympic event in 1964.

あいきどう
合気道

Photo Japan/Kenneth Hamm

The kanji 合 means 'to meet', and 気 means 'spirit'. In 合気道, players train to raise their spiritual awareness and develop physical flexibility. An 合気道 master can 'read' opponents' movements, overwhelming or throwing them by grasping, twisting and applying pressure on their hands, feet and joints, using very little strength. To an observer, a master of 合気道 sometimes appears to be throwing someone without even touching them.

ISBN 9780170196826

しゅみは？

photolibrary

からてどう
空手道

From the original influence of Chinese kung-fu, からて developed from Okinawan martial arts. In からて, a player uses fists, elbows and a kicking action.

からて has two types of しあい (matches): くみて (sparring) and かた (set moves). To win くみて, a player needs to score three points within 3 minutes. One point is awarded each time a punch, strike or kick is performed correctly.

To avoid injury, in modern しあい a player must stop the strike just before it reaches the opponent.

しょどう
書道

しょどう
書道 is the art of writing with a brush and ink. This art form expresses the calligrapher's spirit and demonstrates their skill through the beauty of their written characters and their control of the thickness, shape and intensity of their brush strokes.

In the art of 書道, it is important to maintain good posture and to focus the mind on the meanings and the shape of the characters being written.

In modern Japanese life, brush-and-ink calligraphy is not as common as it used to be; however, many people still use traditional calligraphy for writing New Year's cards, and 書道 is still taught in primary and junior high schools. Students throughout Japan can also attend private calligraphy classes and join their school's calligraphy club.

Corbis

かどう
華道

Flower arranging developed into an art form after the arrival of Buddhism (in AD 538) as people arranged flowers to offer to Buddha.

In 華道, which is also known as いけばな, flowers are arranged to express the three elements of heaven, earth and mankind, and to give a beautiful and a balanced composition.

しゅみは?

ISBN 9780170196826

茶道(さどう)

Corbis

茶道(さどう) originated in China. It was later developed into its current form in the sixteenth century by a man named Sen no Rikyu. Rikyu based 茶道(さどう) around the Zen concepts of わび and さび (subtle taste and simple beauty), and 一期一会(いちごいちえ) (one life, one meeting). Each meeting is unique and must therefore be cherished.

The essence of 茶道(さどう) is to make guests feel special by showing sincerity and attention to detail. The tea ceremony host will water the pathway to the tea room and decorate the tea room using specially arranged flowers and a calligraphy scroll. Special spring water, tea and sweets are also chosen. Special cups are used in the artistic making and offering of tea.

Have a think

8.1

1   Do you know anyone who has tried or seen けんどう, じゅうどう, あいきどう, からて, しょどう, いけばな or さどう?
2   Can you think of examples from your own culture in which a hobby or activity has become someone's lifetime pursuit?

Have a go

1   Try しょどう, さどう or いけばな.
2   Research one of the Japanese sports or traditional arts described, and find out if there are any masters or clubs in your area.

08

百
四
十
九

149

ISBN 9780170196826

しゅみは?

うたいましょう

The hobbies song

Say this song in a rap style, and clap along.

しゅみは
なんですか
スポーツ
おんがく
コンピューター
ラグビー
サッカー、 スキー
ダンス、 ゴルフ
りょうーーーーり

The every day rap

Do this rap with rap actions.

まいにち、	(fists closed, swing around)
いつも、	(punches in the air)
よく、	(fists closed, elbows tucked in to sides)
ときどき、	(flap wings)
あまり、	(straight hand, あまり gesture)
ぜんぜん、	(fists closed, arms making a cross)
〜ません。	(hands flip down and up)

How often?

What do we need to remember? まいにち, いつも, よく and ときどき need ます. However, あまり and ぜんぜん need ません.

おりがみ

かぶと

A かぶと is a type of helmet that was worn by さむらい in feudal Japan. These days decorative helmets are displayed in the homes of boys for Children's Day on 5 May. Ask your teacher for the instructions on how to make an origami かぶと.

すもう

Make origami sumo wrestlers, then use them in your own sumo match. Ask your teacher for the instructions.

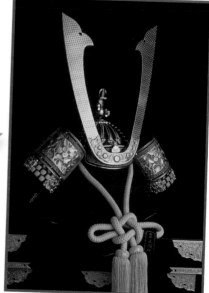

ISBN 9780170196826

おしょうゆ

Here are some useful expressions from いただきます.

よかった！
That was good!

でも
but

きて　ください。
Please come.

ちょっと
little bit

これは　なん　ですか。
What is this?

しんじられない！
That's unbelievable!
ほんとう？
Really?

よいしょ！　よいしょ！
Push! Heave!
(Use this expression when you are lifting or pushing something very heavy.)

たいへん！
Oh no!
ざんねん　ですね。
Bad luck!
That's a pity!

おつかれさま！
Thanks for your hard work!
(You say this to people who might be tired after doing something for you.)

おめでとう！ Look at all of the things you have learnt in this unit!
Go to your workbook and fill in the checklist at the end of the unit.

やっぱり、　ゆうすけは　すてき！
Just as I thought! Yuusuke, you are so cool!

08

百
五
十
一

151

ISBN 9780170196826

しゅみは？

Unit 9

どこに？ だれと？ なんで？

どこに？ だれと？ なんで？

どこに？ だれと？ なんで？

ISBN 9780170196826

Have a think ○○○○○○○○○○○○○○○○○○○○○○○○○○○○○○

1 What do you say in Japanese if you arrive late?
2 What are two ways of saying 'sorry' in Japanese?
3 Why can they not have the party on Friday?
4 Where is Tony going on Saturday? Who is he going with? How is he getting there?
5 Who else cannot go to the party if it is on Saturday? Where are they going?
6 What gesture does Yuki make to get everyone to be quiet? Would you do the same thing?
7 Listen to the *manga* again and see if you can work out how to ask:
   • where someone is going
   • who someone is going with
   • how someone is getting there.

どんなあじ?

Asking where someone is going on the weekend and responding

しゅうまつに　どこに　いきますか。

うみに　いきます。

しゅうまつに　どこに　いきますか。

えいがに　いきます。

しゅうまつに　どこに　いきますか。

しゅうまつに　まちに　いきます。

ロールプレー

A	しゅうまつに　どこに　いきますか。	
B	□に　いきます。	□さんは? □くんは?
A	□に　いきます。	

Asking who someone is going with and responding

だれと　いきますか。

ゆうすけくんと　いきます。

だれと　いきますか。

ゆきさんと　いきます。

だれと　いきますか。

一人で　いきます。

09

百五十六

156

どこに? だれと? なんで?

ISBN 9780170196826

The せつめい pages at the back of this book will give you even more information to help you talk about where you are going, who you are going with and how you are getting there. Just turn to page 228.

ロールプレー

A	しゅうまつに　どこに　いきますか。		
B	☐に　いきます。		
A	だれと　いきますか。		
B	☐と　いきます。	☐さんは ☐くんは	どこに　いきますか。
A	☐に　いきます。		
B	だれと　いきますか。		
A	☐と　いきます。		

Asking how someone is getting there and responding

なんで　いきますか。

でんしゃで　いきます。

なんで　いきますか。

あるいて　いきます。

なんで　いきますか。

<ruby>ばす<rt></rt></ruby>バスで　いきます。

ロールプレー

A	しゅうまつに　どこに　いきますか。		
B	☐に　いきます。		
A	なんで　いきますか。		
B	☐で　いきます。	☐さんは ☐くんは	どこに　いきますか。
A	☐に　いきます。		
B	なんで　いきますか。		
A	☐で　いきます。		

09

百
五
十
七

157

ISBN 9780170196826

どこに？ だれと？ なんで？

つくりましょう！

Text message

Yuusuke and Kate are going out together on Saturday!
They have each written text messages to their friends to tell
them what they are going to do. What sort of day do you
think they have planned? Read their messages to find out.

ゆきさんへ
ねえ、きいて。😀 土曜日（どようび）に
コンサートに　いきます。🎵 あらしの
コンサート　ですよ。　すごいね。
ゆうすけくんと　くるまで　いきます。😀
そして、　まちに　いきます。
イタリア（いたりあ）の　レストラン（れすとらん）に
いきます。　チキン（ちきん）と　パスタ（ぱすた）を
たべます。　そして、🍰 ケーキ（けーき）を
たべます。　おいしい　ですよ。
あとで　デパート（でぱーと）に　いきます。
かいものを　します。　かいものが
だいすき 🩷 ですよ。　たのしみー。
ケイト（けいと）より

ベンくんへ
きいて　ください。　土曜日（どようび）に 🥚
ケイト（けいと）さんと　コンサートに
いきます。🎵 あらしの　コンサート（こんさーと）
ですよ。😀 ぼくは　あらしが　すき
じゃない　ですよ。　バス（ばす）で
いきます。　そして、　マクドナルド（まくどなると）に
いきます。　チーズバーガーコンボ（ちーずばーがーこんぼ）を
たべます。　ぼくは　ハンバーガー（はんばーがー）が
だいすき 🩷 です。　そして、
コーラ（こーら）を　のみます。　あとで、
ラグビー（らぐびー）の　しあいに　いきます。
すごいね。
ゆうすけより

Have a go

1　Using these text messages as a guide, write a text
message to your friend telling them what you plan
to do on the weekend. Start with your friend's name,
followed by へ; this means 'to' or 'dear'. End your
message with your name followed by より; this means
'from'. In the message, write about:

- what you are going to do
- where you are going
- who you are going with
- how you are going to get there
- what you plan to eat or drink.

Useful words

かいもの	shopping
あとで	later
すき　じゃない	do not like
そして	and
それから	and then
でも	but
ときどき	sometimes
しゅうまつに	on the weekend

どこに？ だれと？ なんで？

ISBN 9780170196826

カタカナ

Use the chart to say the *katakana* sounds. Your teacher will help you.

*	w	r	y	m	h	n	t	s	k	
ン n	ワ	ラ	ヤ	マ	ハ	ナ	タ	サ	カ	ア	a
		リ		ミ	ヒ	ニ	チ chi	シ shi	キ	イ	i
		ル	ユ	ム	フ fu	ヌ	ツ tsu	ス	ク	ウ	u
		レ		メ	ヘ	ネ	テ	セ	ケ	エ	e
	ヲ	ロ	ヨ	モ	ホ	ノ	ト	ソ	コ	オ	o

Here are the *katakana* introduced in this unit.

ロ ro   ム mu   ナ na   セ se   ウ u

ド do   デ de

Then, use the look, think and count method to see if you can read these words.

ウィークエンド	スポーツ　センター	ディズニーランド	ゲーム
デパート	レストラン	パーティー	コンサート	タクシー
ロック　コンサート	ピクニック	フェリー	スクーター	バス

09

百五十九

ISBN 9780170196826

どこに？ だれと？ なんで？

ごはんとおかず

ごはん

9.5

Shutterstock.com/Tristan Scholze

Asking where someone is going on the weekend and responding

しゅうまつに　どこに　いきますか。
Where are you going on the weekend?
うみに　いきます。 やきゅうの　しあいに　いきます。
I am going to the beach. I am going to a baseball game.

Asking who someone is going with and responding

だれと　いきますか。
Who are you going with?
ゆうすけくんと　いきます。 かぞくと　いきます。 一人で　いきます。
I am going with Yuusuke. I am going with my family. I am going by myself.

Asking how someone is getting there and responding

なんで　いきますか。
By what means are you getting there? (How are you getting there?)
じてんしゃで　いきます。 あるいて　いきます。
I am going by bicycle. I am going on foot.

Photo Japan/Kenneth Hamm

09

百六十

160

どこに？ だれと？ なんで？

ISBN 9780170196826

おかず 9.1, 9.2, 9.3

Places and activities

Core

どこ	where
えいが	movie
うみ	beach
がっこう	school
まち	town
デパート	department store
レストラン	restaurant
コンサート	concert
ピクニック	picnic
パーティー	party
しあい	game; match
うち	house; home

More

テニスの　しあい	a tennis match
フットボールの　しあい	a football match
からての　しあい	a karate match
やきゅうの　しあい	a baseball match
おばあさんの　うち	grandmother's house
ともだちの　うち	friend's house

Conjunctions

More

そして	and
それから	and then
でも	but
ときどき	sometimes

People you go with

Core

だれ	who
かぞく	family
ともだち	friend
一人で	by myself

Means of transport

Core

ひこうき	aeroplane
バス	bus
じてんしゃ	bicycle
でんしゃ	train
タクシー	taxi
しんかんせん	bullet train
フェリー	ferry
スクーター	scooter
あるいて	on foot
くるま	car

More

おかあさんの　くるま	mum's car
ふね	ship
ともだちの　ボート	friend's boat
ヨット	yacht

Verbs

Core

いきます	go
いきません	do not go

ISBN 9780170196826

どこに? だれと? なんで?

テーブルマナー

しんかんせん

The first Japanese しんかんせん (bullet train) line was constructed in 1964. The top speed of the fastest bullet train – the Hayabusa on the Tokaido Line – is 300 kilometres per hour. When it is travelling at this speed, it takes 3 minutes and 45 seconds just to stop! Trains run approximately every 5 minutes.

Photo Japan/Kenneth Hamm

The Joetsu bullet train connects Tokyo with Niigata. The journey takes about 2 hours.

The Tokaido bullet train travels from Tokyo to Osaka (via Kyoto) and takes 2.5 hours.

Shutterstock.com/John Leung

The Sanyo bullet train travels between Osaka and Fukuoka. From Tokyo, the journey to Fukuoka takes 5 hours.

iStockphoto

The Kyushu bullet train travels between Fukuoka and Kagoshima on the island of Kyushu. The northern part of the line was opened in 2011. An extension to Nagasaki is planned.

Kyoto

Nagoya

Osaka

Hiroshima

Fukuoka

Nagasaki

Kagoshima

どこに? だれと? なんで?

ISBN 9780170196826

The Tohoku bullet train travels north from Tokyo to Shin-Aomori. This line has four types of bullet train. The fastest is the Hayabusa, which goes all the way to Shin-Aomori in little more than 3 hours. The Hayate stops more often; the Yamabiko stops even more frequently; and the Nasuno is like a fast, local train.

Getty Images

The Akita bullet train is an extension of the Tohoku bullet train and travels from Morioka to Akita.

Photo Japan/Kenneth Hamm

Shutterstock.com/Thomas Nord

The Yamagata bullet train travels between Tokyo and Yamagata, and takes about 3 hours.

Aomori
Hachinohe
Akita
Morioka
Yamagata
Sendai
Niigata
Nagano
Tokyo

The Nagano bullet train travels between Tokyo and Nagano and takes about 2 hours.

Have a think

1 Do you know the names of other fast trains around the world?
2 Do you prefer travelling by train or by aeroplane? Why?
3 Why do you think it is often more convenient in Japan to travel by bullet train than by aeroplane?
4 Do you think that a fast train network like this would work in Australia? Which routes would be the most popular in Australia?
5 Go online to access Japan's bullet train timetable. Use the timetables and answer the following questions.
   • What are the names of the trains on each line?
   • Which are the fastest?
   • How frequently do they run?

09

百六十三

163

ISBN 9780170196826

どこに？ だれと？ なんで？

Most busy train lines in Japan have three types of trains, each with a different stopping pattern. Journeys to stations where the slowest trains stop can be made quicker by travelling part of the journey on a faster or express train.

Japanese public transport almost always runs on time. The trains are extremely punctual – so much so that if a train is ever running late, passengers are issued with a late note for their school or employer!

Robert Simons

If you are travelling in Japan, you can travel more cheaply on the bullet trains by purchasing a Japan Rail Pass, or JR Pass. These special tickets entitle you to unlimited travel on Japan Rail's national train network, including on the bullet trains, for 7, 14 or 21 days.

Have a think ○○○○○○○○○○○○○○○○○○○○○○○○○○

1   Do some research to find out the distance between Tokyo and Hiroshima. How long does the journey take? Compare the travel time with similar distances in Australia.

Have a go ○○○○○○○○○○○○○○○○○○○○○○○○○○○○○○○○

1   Try planning a trip. You want to go from Tokyo to Kokura, and plan to leave Tokyo around 9 a.m. on Saturday. Use the online timetables to find out which trains to catch, where to change and what time you will arrive.

どこに? だれと? なんで?

ISBN 9780170196826

9.4

うたいましょう

The 'what are we doing?' song

Sing this song to the tune of 'Following the Leader'.

なにを　しますか
しますか
しますか
なにを　しますか
<ruby>金<rt>きんようび</rt></ruby>曜日に

なにを　しますか
しますか
しますか
なにを　しますか
<ruby>日<rt>にちようび</rt></ruby>曜日に

えいがに　いきます
いきます
いきます
えいがに　いきます
<ruby>金<rt>きんようび</rt></ruby>曜日に

うみに　いきます
いきます
いきます
うみに　いきます
<ruby>日<rt>にちようび</rt></ruby>曜日に

なにを　しますか
しますか
しますか
なにを　しますか
<ruby>土<rt>どようび</rt></ruby>曜日に

なにを　しますか
しますか
しますか
なにを　しますか
<ruby>月<rt>げつようび</rt></ruby>曜日に

<ruby>パーティー<rt>ぱーてぃー</rt></ruby>に　いきます
いきます
いきます
<ruby>パーティー<rt>ぱーてぃー</rt></ruby>に　いきます
<ruby>土<rt>どようび</rt></ruby>曜日に

がっこうに　いきます
いきます
いきます
がっこうに　いきます
<ruby>月<rt>げつようび</rt></ruby>曜日に

Shutterstock.com/wdeon

09

百六十五

165

ISBN 9780170196826

どこに？ だれと？ なんで？

Particles

One way to tell what a sentence is about is to look at the *hiragana* characters that appear at the end of the key words. Because of their position, these characters are sometimes called post-positions. They are also often called particles.

Where are the particles in these sentences? What does each sentence mean?

- わたし**は**　たかこ　です。
- わたし**は**　にく**を**　たべます。
- でんしゃ**で**　いきます。
- ペット**が**　います。
- しゅうまつ**に**　うみ**に**　いきます。
- レストラン**に**　いきます。
- けんいちくん**の**　いぬ　です。
- おかあさん**と**　いきます。

Have a think

1　Each particle gives a different clue. In which sentence does the particle provide a clue about:

- the person I am going with?
- the place I am going to?
- who the pet belongs to?
- the person I am telling you about?
- whether I have a pet?
- what I eat?
- the date or day I am doing an activity?
- the means of transport used to get to a place?

Some particles have particular meanings, like と, の, に and で. Other particles have particular purposes, like は, が and を.

Particles are 'linked' to the word they follow. You will know more about what the particle is doing by looking at the word before it. This is much the same as looking at the word before an apostrophe to see what the apostrophe refers to (for example, Kenichi's).

What if you are not sure which particle to use? If someone asks you a question and you are not sure which particle to use in your reply, ask the person to repeat the question again. Listen carefully for the question words, such as なん, なに, だれ, どこ and いつ. Then, replace the question word with your answer and use the same particles. For example:

- **どこ**に　いきますか。(question)
  うみに　いきます。(answer)
- **なん**で　いきますか。(question)
  くるまで　いきます。(answer)
- **だれ**と　いきますか。(question)
  ともだちと　いきます。(answer)
- **なに**を　のみますか。(question)
  みずを　のみます。(answer)

Shutterstock.com

どこに？だれと？なんで？

ISBN 9780170196826

おしょうゆ

9.7

Here are some useful expressions from いただきます.

みなさんへ
to everyone
dear everyone

きょうしつに きて ください。
Please come to the classroom.

ゆき より
from Yuki

ひみつ です。
It is a secret.

ごめんなさい。
I'm sorry.
I apologise.

すみません!
I'm sorry!
Excuse me!

おそく なって、 すみません!
Sorry I am late!

おそーい!
Late!

はやく はいって!
Quick, come in!

かいぎを します。
I will start the meeting.

おめでとう! Look at all of the things you have learnt in this unit! Go to your workbook and fill in the checklist at the end of the unit.

日曜日は いい?
Is Sunday okay?

だめ!
Not good!

はい、 いい です。
Yes, it is okay.

いいよ!
Good!
Okay!

だいじょうぶよ!
It's all right!

09

百六十七

167

ISBN 9780170196826

どこに? だれと? なんで?

Unit 10

クラブかつどう

ISBN 9780170196826

1 In Japan, many students are involved in club activities. Do you have club activities at your school? What are the benefits of club activities?
2 What four activities does Yuusuke's club do?
3 List four activities that Yuki's club does.
4 What is コスプレ?
5 What activities have been arranged for the computer club and when are they scheduled?
6 What club does Takako belong to?
7 What do you think the cultural festival is like? Do you have a similar day in your school?

10

百
七
十
一

171

クラブかつどう

Asking about daily activities and responding

ISBN 9780170196826

ロールプレー	
A	なにを　しますか。
B	☐を　たべます。
	☐を　のみます。
	☐を　みます。
	☐を　ききます。
	☐を　かきます。
	☐を　よみます。
	☐を　かいます。
	☐を　とります。
	☐を　します。
	☐を　つくります。
	☐に　いきます。
	☐に　あいます。
	ねます。

Talking about daily activities you do or do not do

ざっしを よみますか。

はい、 ざっしを よみます。

おんがくを ききますか。

いいえ、 おんがくを ききません。

テレビを みます。

しゅくだいを しません。

ロールプレー

A		□を □ますか。	
B	はい、	□を □ます。 □に いきます。 □に あいます。 ねます。	
	いいえ、	□を □ません。 □に いきません。 □に あいません。 ねません。	

The せつめい pages at the back of this book will give you even more information to help you talk about what you do and do not do. Just turn to page 229.

Letter

Thomas is going to stay with Masahiro during the school holidays as part of his school trip to Japan. They have exchanged letters before. Now, Masahiro is writing to tell Thomas about his hobbies.

トーマスくんへ、
こんにちは。 おげんき ですか。 ぼくは げんき です。
きょうは ぼくの しゅみに ついて かきます。

ぼくの しゅみは スポーツと おんがく です。

おとうさんは けんどうの せんせい です。 だから、 金曜日に
おとうさんと けんどうを します。 トーマスくんは けんどうが

できますか。
それから、 月曜日と 水曜日に やきゅうを します。 土曜日に
やきゅうの しあいに いきます。 やきゅうが だいすき です。
やきゅうの ざっしを よみます。
そして、 あとで、 ともだちと スタバ(Starbucks)に いきます。
コーヒーを のみます。 エクストラ コーヒー ビター
キャラメル フラペチーノが だいすき です! おいしい
ですよ!
ウェブサイトを みて ください!
おんがくも だいすき です。 J-popを ききます。 ときどき
コンサートに いきますよ。
トーマスくんは スカイプが できますか。
じゃあ、 またね。 **へんじを ください。**
まさひろ より

Useful words

だから	therefore
あとで	afterwards

Speech

In some ways, writing a speech is like writing a letter, but speeches have different expressions that you use to begin and end the speech and introduce the topic.

ISBN 9780170196826

Letter

In the beginning of a letter, use expressions like:

- はじめまして。How do you do? (Used in a letter of introduction.)
- おげんき　ですか。How are you?
- わたしは　げんき　です。I am well.
- ひさしぶり　ですね。Long time no see.

Introducing the topic:

- きょうは　□に　ついて　かきます。Today, I am writing about …

Here are some handy expressions to use at the end of a letter:

- へんじを　ください。Please reply.
- てがみを　かいて　ください。Please write back.
- おへんじを　まって　います。I will be waiting for your reply.
- じゃあ、　また　てがみを　かきます。Well, I will write to you again.

Speech

In the beginning of a speech, it is usual to use expressions like:

- みなさん、　こんにちは。Hello, everyone.
- せんせい、　せいとの　みなさん、　こんにちは。
  Hello, teachers and students.

You introduce a new topic in a speech by saying:

- きょうは　□に　ついて　はなします。
  Today, I am speaking about …
  (For example, きょうは　しゅみに　ついて　はなします。
  Today, I am speaking about hobbies.)

If you are making a speech, end with:

- みなさん、　ありがとう　ございます。Thank you, everyone.
- これで　おわります。That is all for now.
- さいご　まで、　きいて　くれて　ありがとう　ございます。
  Thank you for listening to me until the end.

Ioan-Liviu Orletchi

Have a think

1 What is the purpose of a letter? Who is the audience?
2 What is the purpose of a speech? Who is the audience?
3 a Which sentences in the letter opposite would not be appropriate for a speech?
   b Identify the conjunctions (linking words). How do they improve the text?

Have a go

1 Write a letter to a Japanese friend telling him or her about your hobbies.
2 Write the script of a speech that you could give at your sister school about your favourite pastime.

ISBN 9780170196826

クラブかつどう

べんきょうのベン

カタカナ

Use the chart to say the *katakana* sounds. Your teacher will help you.

*	w	r	y	m	h	n	t	s	k		
ン n	ワ	ラ	ヤ	マ	ハ	ナ	タ	サ	カ	ア	a
		リ		ミ	ヒ	ニ	チ chi	シ shi	キ	イ	i
		ル	ユ	ム	フ fu	ヌ	ツ tsu	ス	ク	ウ	u
		レ		メ	ヘ	ネ	テ	セ	ケ	エ	e
	ヲ	ロ	ヨ	モ	ホ	ノ	ト	ソ	コ	オ	o

Here are the *katakana* introduced in this unit.

 ヨ yo ユ yu モ mo メ me ヌ nu

ワ wa

The *katakana* for を is ヲ; however, because sentences are no longer written in *katakana*, ヲ is no longer used.

クラブかつどう

ISBN 9780170196826

Use the look, think and count method to see if you can read these words, which include many technology terms.

ホームルーム　メール　ビデオ　ソフト

ファッションざっし　ビデオクリップ　テレビ　ラジオ

アニメ　カラオケ　ウェブサイト　ワイヤレス

ホームページ　ケイタイサイト　アカウント　アプリケーション

ブックマーク　キャンセル　コンピューター　ダウンロード

ファイル　フォルダー　ヘルプ　ホーム　インターネット

ログイン　ログアウト　メモリー　メニュー　オンライン

スクリーンショット　スタート　タブ　ウィキペディア

Can you read these signs?

ISBN 9780170196826

クラブかつどう

10.5

クラブかつどう（ぶかつ）

In Japan, students are encouraged to participate in after-school club activities, which are called クラブかつどう or ぶかつ. Club activities are a big part of school life as most clubs meet every day after school to practise.

　　At the beginning of the school year, clubs promote themselves to new students. Each year they set up stalls during school sporting events and for the ぶんかさい (cultural festival). There is keen competition between members of different clubs.

　　The せんぱい〜こうはい (senior–junior) system is also very important. こうはい (junior students) must show respect to their せんぱい (senior students) by bowing and saying こんにちは when they see them in or outside of school. In return, せんぱい commit to looking after their こうはい. For example, if a こうはい is having trouble with teachers or other students, a せんぱい would step in and negotiate on their behalf. They even give こうはい their past class notes and exam papers.

　　There are two types of clubs: たいいくけい (sports clubs) and ぶんかけい (cultural clubs).

たいいくけい (sports clubs)

Photos by Ioan-Liviu Orletchi, Kiewa College, Markane Sipraseuth, Magdy Habib, Cameron Stevens and Christopher Kocx

Other sporting clubs in Japan include:
- バスケットボールぶ (basketball club)
- バレーボールぶ (volleyball club)
- りくじょうぶ (athletics club)
- すいえいぶ (swimming club)
- たっきゅうぶ (table tennis club)

やきゅうぶ
Baseball club

サッカーぶ
Soccer club

テニスぶ
Tennis club

きゅうどうぶ
Japanese archery club

けんどうぶ
Kendo club

10

百七十八

178

ISBN 9780170196826

ぶんかけい (cultural clubs)

えんげきぶ
Drama club

さどうぶ
Tea ceremony club

びじゅつぶ
Visual arts club

Photos by Ioan-Liviu Orletchi

ESS
English-speaking society

Other cultural clubs in Japan include:
- しょどうぶ
  (calligraphy club)
- かがくぶ
  (science club)
- ほうそうぶ
  (broadcasting club)
- すいそうがくぶ
  (symphonic winds club)
- べんろんぶ
  (debating club)
- しゃしんぶ
  (photography club)

This is only a selection of the many, many different clubs at Japanese high schools. Some schools even invent their own new activities and clubs.

Have a think

1 What after-school activities are offered at your school?
2 Do you participate in any club activities in or outside of school?
3 Which Japanese school sports club or cultural club would you like to join? Why?
4 What do you think are the benefits of participating in club activities like these?

Have a go

1 Does your school have a sister school in Japan? If you do, find out what sports and cultural clubs are available to students at your sister school.
2 If your school does not have a connection with a school in Japan, do some research to find a Japanese school's website and read about their after-school club programme.

10

百七十九

179

ISBN 9780170196826

クラブかつどう

うたいましょう

The verbs song

Sing along to the tune of 'Twinkle, Twinkle, Little Star'.

たべ、　のみ、　きき、　み
かき、　よみ、　いき、　し
とります and ねます too
Add a ます
That's all you do
あい、　かい、　つくり
Japanese verbs are so easy!

> 本を　よみません。　ねます。

Corbis/amanaimages

> おかしを　かいます。
> おかしを　たべます。

> おんがくを　ききます。　ゲームを　します。

Corbis/James Leynes

クラブかつどう

ISBN 9780170196826

ごはんとおかず
ごはん

Getty Images

Asking about daily activities and responding

なにを　しますか。
What do you do? What will you do?
すしを　たべます。 みずを　のみます。 えいがを　みます。 おんがくを　ききます。 てがみを　かきます。 ざっしを　よみます。 くつを　かいます。 しゃしんを　とります。 しゅくだいを　します。 ケーキを　つくります。 うみに　いきます。 ともだちに　あいます。 ねます。
I eat sushi. I drink water. I watch (look at) movies. I listen to music. I write letters. I read magazines. I buy shoes. I take pictures. I do homework. I make cakes. I go to the beach. I meet friends. I sleep.

Talking about daily activities you do or do not do

しゅくだいを　します。
I do homework.
えいがを　みません。
I do not watch movies.
ざっしを　よみますか。
Do you read magazines?
はい、　ざっしを　よみます。 いいえ、　ざっしを　よみません。
Yes, I read magazines. No, I do not read magazines.

10.3, 10.4

ISBN 9780170196826

クラブかつどう

10

おかず

10.1

Activity words for **do** or **play**
▭を　します

Core

でんわ	telephone
れんしゅう	practice
べんきょう	study
しゅくだい	homework
パーティー ぱ ー て ぃ ー	party
かいもの	shopping
カラオケ か ら お け	karaoke
チャット ちゃっと	(Internet) chat

More

ピアノの ぴ あ の	れんしゅう	piano practice
バンドの ば ん ど	れんしゅう	band practice
日本ごの に ほん	べんきょう	Japanese study

Activity words for **listen**
▭を　ききます

Core

ラジオ ら じ お	radio
おんがく	music
CD (シーディー) し ー て ぃ ー	CD

More

iPod (アイポッド) あ い ぼっ ど	iPod

Activity words for **write**
▭を　かきます

Core

てがみ	letter
にっき	diary

More

さくぶん	essay; composition

Activity words for **read**
▭を　よみます

Core

本 ほん	book
ざっし	magazine
まんが	comic
しんぶん	newspaper
メール め ー る	email

More

きょうかしょ	textbook
じしょ	dictionary
イーブック い ー ぶっ く	ebook

Activity words for **take**
▭を　とります

Core

しゃしん	photo
ビデオ ひ で お	video

クラブかつどう

ISBN 9780170196826

Activity words for **buy**
□を　かいます

Core

かめら カメラ	camera
くつ	shoes
けいたい	mobile

More

ふく	clothes

Activity words for **make**
□を　つくります

Core

けーき ケーキ	cake
すし	sushi

Activity words for **watch** or **look at**
□を　みます

Core

びでおくりっぷ ビデオクリップ	video clip
でぃーゔぃーでぃー DVD（ディーヴィーディー）	DVD
てれび テレビ	television
えいが	movie
あにめ アニメ	animated movie

More

ふぇいすぶっく フェイスブック	Facebook

Activity words for **meet**
□に　あいます

Core

ともだち	friend
かぞく	family

Core

Verbs		Verbs (negative)	
たべます	eat	たべません	do not eat
のみます	drink	のみません	do not drink
みます	watch; look at	みません	do not watch; do not look at
ききます	listen	ききません	do not listen
かきます	write	かきません	do not write
よみます	read	よみません	do not read
かいます	buy	かいません	do not buy
とります	take; record	とりません	do not take; do not record
します	do; play; hold	しません	do not do; do not play; do not hold
つくります	make	つくりません	do not make
いきます	go	いきません	do not go
あいます	meet	あいません	do not meet
ねます	sleep; lie down	ねません	do not sleep; do not lie down

10

百八十三

ISBN 9780170196826

クラブかつどう

おしょうゆ

Here are some useful expressions from いただきます.

いらっしゃい!
Welcome!
Come in!

えーと
um

それから
and then
そして
and

らぐびー
ラグビーぶ
rugby club
さどうぶ
tea ceremony club

ああ、 そーう?
Oh, is that so? (informal)

へえ、 そーう?
Really, is that right? (informal)

そう ですか。
Is that so?
Is that right? (formal)

おめでとう! Look at all of the things you have learnt in this unit!
Go to your workbook and fill in the checklist at the end of the unit.

10

クラブかつどう

ISBN 9780170196826

ひまなとき

メニュー

ひまなとき

ISBN 9780170196826

ひまなとき

ISBN 9780170196826

Have a think

1 What does Takako do in her spare time?
2 What does Kate do in her spare time?
3 What does Yuki do in her spare time?
4 What does Emma do in her spare time?
5 What was Harjono set on arranging?
6 What did Harjono say about the movie?
7 Why did Harjono thank Yuusuke?

8 Listen to the CD again and see if you can recognise how to say the following:
- What do you do in your spare time?
- Let's watch a movie on Friday after school.
- Let's watch (a movie) together.

どんなあじ?

Asking about free time and responding

ひまな ときに なにを しますか。

おんがくを ききます。

がっこうの まえに なにを しますか。

て れ び
テレビを みます。

がっこうの あとで なにを しますか。

て に す
テニスの れんしゅうを します。

きんようび
金曜日の ばん、なにを しますか。

ともだちに あいます。

よる なにを しますか。

す ぽ ー つ
スポーツの ざっしを よみます。

ロールプレー

A	ひまな ときに やす ひる休みに あさ、	なにを しますか。	
B	□に	□を □ます。	□さんは? □くんは?
A	わたしは ぼくは	ひまな ときに やす ひる休みに あさ、	□を □ます。

11

百
八
十
九

189

ISBN 9780170196826

ひまなとき

Suggesting something and responding

あいすくりーむ
アイスクリームを
たべましょう。

はい、 たべましょう。

じゅーす
いっしょに ジュースを
のみましょう。

はい、 のみましょう。

けーき
ケーキを つくりましょう。

はい、 そう しましょう。

きんようび
金曜日の ばん
まちに いきましょう。

はい、 いきましょう。

がっこうの あとで
しゅくだいを しましょう。

いいえ、 それは ちょっと...

ロールプレー

A	☐に	☐を	☐ましょう。
	☐の まえに	☐に	
	☐の あとで		
	☐の ばん		
	☐の あさ		
B	はい、	☐ましょう。	
		そう しましょう。	
	いいえ、	それは ちょっと...	

ISBN 9780170196826

Expressing opinions and responding

あ い す く り ー む
アイスクリームは
おいしい です。

にほん
日本ごは たのしい ですね。

はい、 たのしい
ですね。

こ ん ぴ ゅ ー た ー
コンピューターは やすい です。

45,000円 45,000円

いいえ、 たかい ですよ。

The **せつめい** pages at the back of
this book will give you even more
information to help you talk about
your free time, make suggestions and
express opinions. Just turn to page 230.

The せつめい pages ... Just turn to page 230.

ロールプレー

A	☐は ☐ ですね。
B	はい、 ☐ ですね。
	いいえ、 ☐ ですよ。

11

百
九
十
一

191

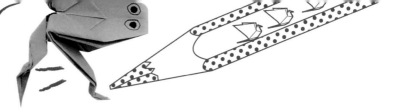

つくりましょう!

Invitation

けんいちくんへ、

11月23日(がつ にち)は ラグビー(らぐびー)の グランドファイナル(ぐらんどふぁいなる) です。

ぼくの チーム(ちーむ)の しあいを みて ください。 ぼくの チーム(ちーむ)は すごい ですよ。

おとうさんは ビデオ(びでお)を とります。 そして、 しあいの あとで、 あいましょう。

バーベキュー(ばーべきゅー)を しますよ。 たのしい ですよ。

ソーセージ(そーせーじ)を たべましょう。 コーラ(こーら)を のみましょう。

おかあさんは ケーキ(けーき)を つくります。 おいしい ですよ。

しあいの あとで、 クラブハウスに きて ください。

ゆうすけ より

たかこさんへ

えいがが すき ですか。 8月15日(がつ にち)は こわい えいが フェスティバル(ふぇすてぃばる) です。 よる、 しぶやシネマ(しねま)に いきましょう。

そして、 こわい えいがを みましょう。 3D ですよ。 こわ〜い。 でも、 おもしろい!

でんしゃで いきましょう。

こわい えいが フェスティバル(ふぇすてぃばる)

8月15日

じかん: 7.30

ばしょ: しぶやシネマ(しねま)

でんわ して ください。

ぼくの でんわ ばんごうは 090-7354-5233 です。

ハジョーノ(はじょーの) より

ISBN 9780170196826

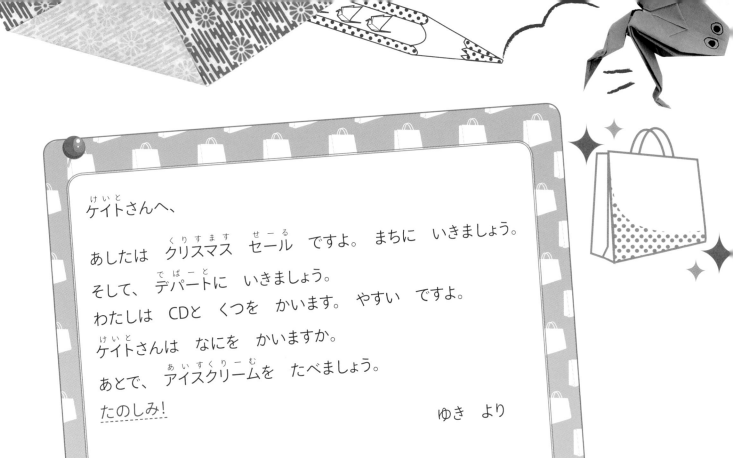

ケイト<ruby>さんへ<rt>けいと</rt></ruby>、

あしたは　<ruby>クリスマス<rt>くりすます</rt></ruby>　<ruby>セール<rt>せーる</rt></ruby>　ですよ。　まちに　いきましょう。

そして、　<ruby>デパート<rt>でぱーと</rt></ruby>に　いきましょう。

わたしは　CDと　くつを　かいます。　やすい　ですよ。

<ruby>ケイト<rt>けいと</rt></ruby>さんは　なにを　かいますか。

あとで、　<ruby>アイスクリーム<rt>あいすくりーむ</rt></ruby>を　たべましょう。

たのしみ!

ゆき　より

Useful words

きて　ください	please come
じかん	time
ばしょ	venue
でんわ　して　ください	please call
たのしみ!	looking forward to it!

Have a go

○○○○○○○○○○○○

1 Using these invitations as a guide, create an invitation
  to your own special event.

ISBN 9780170196826

ひまなとき

カタカナ

Sound changes

In the same way that they change the sounds of *hiragana*, *maru* (゜) and *nigori* (゛) change the sounds of *katakana*.

p	b	h	d	t	z	s	g	k	
パ pa	バ ba	ハ ha	ダ da	タ ta	ザ za	サ sa	ガ ga	カ ka	a
ピ pi	ビ bi	ヒ hi	ヂ ji	チ chi	ジ ji	シ shi	ギ gi	キ ki	i
プ pu	ブ bu	フ fu	ヅ dzu	ツ tsu	ズ zu	ス su	グ gu	ク ku	u
ペ pe	ベ be	ヘ he	デ de	テ te	ゼ ze	セ se	ゲ ge	ケ ke	e
ポ po	ボ bo	ホ ho	ド do	ト to	ゾ zo	ソ so	ゴ go	コ ko	o

Combination sounds

You already know that small *hiragana* や, ゆ and よ are used to create combinations sounds like 'sha', 'shu' and 'sho'. The same thing happens in *katakana*. However, because *katakana* is used for words borrowed from other languages, small ア, イ and エ are also used to reproduce some of the sounds found in languages other than Japanese.

r	m	f	p	b	h	n
リ ri	ミ mi	フ fu	ピ pi	ビ bi	ヒ hi	ニ ni
リャ rya	ミャ mya	ファ fa	ピャ pya	ビャ bya	ヒャ hya	ニャ nya
		フィ fi				
リュ ryu	ミュ myu		ピュ pyu	ビュ byu	ヒュ hyu	ニュ nyu
		フェ fe				
リョ ryo	ミョ myo	フォ fo	ピョ pyo	ビョ byo	ヒョ hyo	ニョ nyo

ひまなとき

ISBN 9780170196826

Small ッ and the dash

The small ツ is used in *katakana* in the same way as it is in *hiragana*. For example:

- バスケットボール
- ネットボール
- インターネット
- サッカー
- ペット

To make sounds long in *katakana* simply add a dash, ー , called a ぼう.

- アイスクリーム
- オレンジジュース
- バレーボール
- コーラ
- コーヒー
- ラグビー

Use the look, think and count method to see if you can read these words and sentences.

サーフィン	パーティー
ファミコン	ウィークエンド
シーディー	ホストファミリー
	ディーヴィーディー

Photos by Magdy Habib, Cameron Stevens and Christopher Kocx

DRINK

- アサヒスーパードライ　500円
- バスペールエール　500円
- オリオンビール　500円
- ジントニック　500円
- カシスオレンジ　500円
- カシスソーダ　500円
- ハイボール　500円
- グアバジュース　300円
- マンゴージュース　300円
- コーラ　250円
- ジンジャーエール　250円
- ピンクレモネード　250円
- オレンジジュース　250円
- アイスティー　250円

	d	t	ch	j	s	g	k	v		
	デ de	テ te	チ chi	ジ ji	シ shi	ギ gi	キ ki	ヴ vu	ウ u	
			チャ cha	ジャ ja	シャ sha	ギャ gya	キャ kya	ヴァ va		ア／ヤ
	ディ di	ティ ti						ヴィ vi	ウィ wi	イ
			チュ chu	ジュ ju	シュ shu	ギュ gyu	キュ kyu			ユ
				ジェ je	シェ she			ヴェ ve	ウェ we	エ
			チョ cho	ジョ jo	ショ sho	ギョ gyo	キョ kyo	ヴォ vo		オ

ごはんとおかず

ごはん

11.2, 11.4

Getty Images

Alamy

Asking about free time and responding

ひまな　ときに がっこうの　あとで 金曜日の　ばん、 あさ、	なにを　しますか。
In your free time, After school, On Friday night, In the morning,	what do you do?
スポーツの　ざっしを　よみます。	
I read sports magazines.	

Suggesting something and responding

ひる休みに あした、	コーヒーを　のみましょう。 パーティーに　いきましょう。
At lunchtime, Tomorrow,	let's drink coffee. let's go to the party.
はい、　たべましょう。 はい、　そう　しましょう。 いいえ、　それは　ちょっと...	
Yes, let's eat. Yes, let's do that. No, I don't really want to.	

Expressing opinions and responding

アイスクリームは　おいしい　です。 えいがは　おもしろい　ですね。
The ice-cream is delicious. The movie is interesting, isn't it?
はい、　たのしい　ですね。 いいえ、　つまらない　ですよ。
Yes, it is fun, isn't it? No, it is boring!

ISBN 9780170196826

おかず

Time expressions

Core

ひまな　ときに	in your spare time
がっこうの　まえに	before school
がっこうの　あとで	after school
あとで	later
ひる休みに	at lunchtime
金曜日の　ばん	Friday evening
あしたの　ばん	tomorrow night
あしたの　あさ	tomorrow morning
あさ	in the morning
よる	at night

'Let's do' verbs

Core

たべましょう	let's eat
のみましょう	let's drink
みましょう	let's watch; let's look
ききましょう	let's listen
かきましょう	let's write
よみましょう	let's read
かいましょう	let's buy
とりましょう	let's take
しましょう	let's do; let's play
つくりましょう	let's make
いきましょう	let's go
あいましょう	let's meet

Photo Japan/Kenneth Hamm

Adjectives

Core

おもしろい	interesting; funny
たのしい	fun
つまらない	boring
おいしい	delicious
まずい	tastes awful
むずかしい	difficult
やさしい	easy
たかい	expensive
やすい	cheap
いい	good

Sentence endings

More

ね	isn't it? (use to confirm)
よ	it is! (use to emphasise)

Together

Core

いっしょに	together

ISBN 9780170196826

ひまなとき

まんが＆アニメ

Japanese *manga* (printed comics) and *anime* (animated films) are taking the world by storm!

The history of *manga* in Japan goes back to the late nineteenth century; however, it was not until the 1970s that Japanese *manga* really took off around the world.

Osamu Tezuka, known as the father of modern *manga*, created *Jungle Emperor, Leo* (also known as *Kimba the White Lion*) in 1950. It was serialised in a magazine called *Manga Shonen*. His most famous *manga*, 「てつわんアトム」 (*Astro Boy*) was first published in Japan in 1952 and shown on Japanese television in 1963. It was remade in the 1980s and again in 2009, as an American computer-animated 3D film.

Popular manga

There are two main types of *manga*: しょうねん and しょうじょ. しょうねん *manga* appeal particularly to boys. They are often about action, fighting and martial arts, and feature a boy as the hero. しょうじょ are *manga* that appeal to girls. The storylines centre around love and teenage romance.

Hayao Miyazaki

Hayao Miyazaki is Japan's best-known *anime* writer and director. He has created many animated feature films such as *Spirited Away* (2001), *Howl's Moving Castle* (2004) and *Ponyo on the Cliff* (2008).

Alamy

ISBN 9780170196826

Alamy

Television series

Many *anime* series appear each day on television in Japan and are extremely popular with adults and children. TV Asahi recently published the 100 most popular *anime* television series in Japan. The top five were:

1   *Fullmetal Alchemist*
2   *Neon Genesis Evangelion*
3   *Pani Poni Dash!*
4   *The Melancholy of Haruhi Suzumiya*
5   *Negima!*

Fan culture

Anime and *manga* are important in Japanese popular culture. It is the whole *manga* experience – the stories and characters, the theme music, the costumes and the merchandise!

For *manga* and *anime* enthusiasts, fan websites open up the world of character information, provide episodes that can be watched online and connect fans to others from around the world. You can learn *manga* language, sing the theme songs (which become hits in their own right), see the episodes as they are released in Japan, and learn to draw your own. There is no excuse for not becoming a *manga* or *anime* おたく(geek)!

Serious fans of *manga* and *anime* meet at parties and trade shows, and dress up as their favourite *manga* characters. This is known as こすぷれ コスプレ, which is short for 'costume play'.

Ioan-Liviu Orletchi

Have a think ○○○○○○○○○○○○○○○○○○○○○○○○

1   In what ways are Japanese *manga* and cartoons from other countries similar? How are they different?
2   Why do you think *anime* and *manga* are so popular worldwide?

Have a go ○○○○○○○○○○○○○○○○○○○○○○○○

1   Try to find copies of Japanese *manga*. How would you describe the characters and images in boys' and girls' *manga*?
2   Check out some of Hayao Miyazaki's movies and some of the other popular television series on the Internet.

ISBN 9780170196826

ひまなとき

うたいましょう

Ioan-Liviu Orletchi

♪ Let's!

Sing along with the Obento CDs. You can use the tune for all the verses.

Verse 1

ひまな　ときには
なにを　しますか
ともだちに
でんわを　しましょう
月曜日に
がっこうの　あとで
テレビを　みましょう

Chorus

まいにち、　たのしい　たのしい
まいにち、　おもしろい

Verse 2

ひまな　ときには
なにを　しますか
ともだちに
でんわを　しましょう
火曜日に
がっこうの　あとで
テニスを　しましょう

Verse 3

ひまな　ときには
なにを　しますか
ともだちに
でんわを　しましょう
水曜日に
がっこうの　あとで
ＣＤを　ききましょう

Chorus

まいにち、　たのしい　たのしい
まいにち、　おもしろい

Verse 4

ひまな　ときには
なにを　しますか
ともだちに
でんわを　しましょう
木曜日に
がっこうの　あとで
ピザを　たべましょう

Verse 5

ひまな　ときには
なにを　しますか
ともだちに
でんわを　しましょう
金曜日に
がっこうの　あとで
パーティーに　いきましょう
パーティーに　いきましょう
パーティーに　いきましょう
パーティーに　いきましょう

ISBN 9780170196826

おしょうゆ

11.3, 11.5

Here are some useful expressions from いただきます。

いつも
always

ちょっと まって!
Wait a minute!

いっしょに
together

I ♥ アニメ

おめでとう! Look at all of the things you have learnt in this unit! Go to your workbook and fill in the checklist at the end of the unit.

ISBN 9780170196826

ひまなとき

Unit 12

どうでしたか

どうでしたか

どうでしたか

ISBN 9780170196826

1   What do you notice about the Japanese inn?
2   What did they do after breakfast?
3   What did they do next? Did Kenichi have his camera then?
4   What did they do after that? Did Kenichi have his camera then? What do you
    notice about Japanese people when they have their photos taken?
5   Where did they go next?
6   Where did Kenichi end up finding his camera?
7   Listen to the CD again and see if you can recognise how to say:
    • Did you take a photo?
    • Yes, I took a photo.
    • No, I did not take a photo.

12

二
百
五

205

ISBN 9780170196826

どうでしたか

Asking what someone did and responding

ロールプレー

A	□に きのう、	なにを しましたか。
B	□を □ました。 □に □ました。	□さんは? □くんは?
A	わたしは ぼくは	□を □ました。 □に □ました。

Talking about what you did and did not do

ISBN 9780170196826

きのう、 パーティーに いきましたか。

はい、 パーティーに いきました。

きのう、 ともだちに あいましたか。

いいえ、 ともだちに あいませんでした。

ロールプレー

A	□を □ましたか。	
B	はい、□を □ました。	□さんは?
	いいえ、□を □ませんでした。	□くんは?
A	わたしは □を □ました。	
	ぼくは □に □ました。	

Asking what something was like and responding

りょこうは どう でしたか。

たのしかった です。

おこのみやきは どう でしたか。

おいしかった です。

えいがは どう でしたか。

おもしろかった です。

ロールプレー

A	□は どう でしたか。
B	□は □かった です。

The せつめい pages at the back of this book will give you even more information to help you talk about what you did and what things were like in the past. Just turn to page 231.

Just turn to page 231.

12

二百七

. . . .

207

ISBN 9780170196826

どうでしたか

つくりましょう！

Recount

Naomi is talking about what she did at the cultural festival.

みなさん、　こんにちは。

きょうは　ぶんかさいに　ついて　はなします。

11月14日に　ぶんかさいを　しました。　ぶんかさいは
たのしかった　ですよ。

わたしの　クラスは　「シスターアクト」の　ドラマを
しました。　おかしかった　です。

ぶんぺいくんは　コンサートを　しましたよ。　ギターが
できますよ。　すごかった　です。　だから、　しゃしんを
とりました。

そして、　のぞみさんは　からての　デモンストレーションを
しました。　よかった　ですよ。　びっくり　しました。

みかさんの　クラブは　ビンテージセールを　しました。
ＣＤは　やすかった　です。　だから、　ＣＤを
かいました。　でも、　まんがは　たかかった　です。
だから、　かいませんでした。

コンピューター　クラブは　クッキーを　つくりました。
でも、　クッキーは　まずかった　ですよ。

マイクくんの　クラスは　やきとりを　つくりました。
やきとりは　おいしかった　です。

わたしの　けんどう　クラブは　おばけやしきを　しました。

わたしは　ドラキュラ　でした。　こわかった　ですよ。

ぶんかさいは　ほんとうに　おもしろかった　です。

どうでしたか

ISBN 9780170196826

12.8

Useful words

☐に　ついて　はなします	I will talk about ☐
だから	therefore
びっくり　しました	I was surprised
ビンテージセール	vintage sale
でも	but
おばけやしき	ghost house; haunted house
ドラキュラ　でした	I was Dracula
ほんとうに	really

Have a think

1 What do you notice about the sentences used in the recount?
2 When writing a recount, you need a good mix of fact and opinion. Which words tell you fact (what happened), and which words give opinions (how Naomi felt)?
3 What does the past tense of Japanese verbs end in?
4 What does the past form of Japanese adjectives end in?

Have a go

1 Create a bulletin board for your classroom. Think about an event that happened at school in the last term (such as an excursion, a fête, a big sports match or a party). Write a news bulletin of the things that happened, including what it was like.
2 Use Naomi's recount as a guide to write your own recount of an event you enjoyed this year.

Getty Images

12

二百九

209

どうでしたか

ISBN 9780170196826

わたしたちのがっこうの一年（いちねん）

> It has been a big year for the students at our school. Since the school year began in April, we have had a number of special events in the school calendar. Let's take a look at the year we had.

4月3日
にゅうがくしき

はる休み（やす） was over, and everyone was looking forward to starting the new school year, making new friends, seeing old ones, finding out which classes they would be in and, most of all, checking out the new teachers!

The day started with the にゅうがくしき (school entrance ceremony) where the principal welcomed the new 一（いち）ねんせい and then went on for what seemed like forever about school rules and responsibilities and all that stuff.

Oh well, 一（いち）がっき had started, we just had to make it through to Golden Week!

We have lots of fun memories of the school camp – the campfires, songs and ghost stories after dark. The memory I am trying to forget is the taste of the burnt ごはん that the boys cooked. I guess they were so busy making a campfire, they forgot a bit about the cooking!

5月16日
きゃんぷ
キャンプ

7月21日〜8月31日
なつ休み（やす）

Five weeks holiday! Yes!!!

どうでしたか

ISBN 9780170196826

12.9

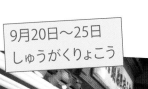

9月20日～25日
しゅうがくりょこう

On 9月20日, we boarded the しんかんせん (bullet train) for Hiroshima. Our aim was to complete our history assignment in five days and still have time to check out the shops.

We stayed in a りょかん (Japanese-style inn) and set off early each morning to visit the famous places of Hiroshima and Miyajima. It seemed that everywhere we went we had a class photo taken. We used our mobile phones to take lots of photos of everyone too.

さん
三りんしゃきょうそう
Tricycle race

10月12日
うんどうかい

Practice began in early September, every afternoon until 5.30 p.m. We stayed later for practice in the last few weeks and practised in the mornings as well. We were so desperate to win after being beaten by あおぐみ (blue team) last year by one point! This year, we even went down to our local shrine, たかやま　じんじゃ, the day before to pray for strength.

Kuri had the bright idea that if we all ate とんかつ (crumbed and deep-fried pork) for dinner the night before the うんどうかい , we would win. He said it was because かつ means 'win'. Of course we ate it! We were not leaving anything to chance. Anyway, I like とんかつ, so I did not mind. It turned out that it was not such a silly idea after all. I'll let the score sheet tell the story.

むかできょうそう
Centipede race
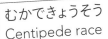

つなひき
Tug of war

Photos by Getty Images, Shutterstock.com, Markane Sipraseuth, Robert Simons

12

二百十一

ISBN 9780170196826

どうでしたか

It was a race between all the clubs! From the right:
テニスぶ、　たっきゅうぶ、　ラグビーぶ、　けんどうぶ、　やきゅうぶ、
りくじょうぶ、　サッカーぶ、　すいえいぶ、　みんな、　がんばって!

やきゅうぶが
かちました。

ふふふ...
やきゅうぶは
すごい!

あっ、　だめ!

	あかぐみ	しろぐみ	あおぐみ	きいろぐみ	ピンクぐみ
100メートルきょうそう	12	18	14	10	13
400メートルきょうそう	17	16	15	11	9
パンくいきょうそう	24	27	28	30	33
かいものきょうそう	20	30	25	24	31
にんげんピラミッド	18	30	29	22	20
つなひき	20	30	25	15	10
むかできょうそう	20	24	29	27	26
三りんしゃきょうそう	29	30	27	26	20
ダンス	27	29	30	26	28
おうえん	27	30	28	26	27
リレー	37	40	38	34	31
	251	304	288	251	248

What a day that was! On the day of the cultural festival, we were all at school at 7.15 a.m. to set up our club stalls. By 8 a.m. the school was full of students and teachers putting up food stalls, games stalls and signs everywhere.

At 9 a.m. the entertainment started. Most of the classes had organised entertainment. Out homeroom class put on a show with Japanese dance, songs and a type of comedy called まんざい (comic dialogue). The room was full of people and we were nervous, but doing the show was fun. We had to look after the tennis-club stall for an hour in the afternoon, but after that we got to look around at all the games and stalls. The best was the おばけやしき (haunted house).

11月14日
ぶんかさい

どうでしたか

ISBN 9780170196826

2月
しけん

しけんは
どう　でしたか。

むずかしかった
です。

The first exam for the year is the worst. I think it is because after the holidays I forget how to do them! Of course, by the end of the year I remember. With the mid-term and end-of-term exams in every term, how could I not?! At least we only have exams in some subjects at mid-term.

3月
そつぎょうしき

The end of the year finally arrived! As we filed into the assembly hall for the final time this year, it seemed like no time since we had been sitting in the にゅうがくしき (school entrance ceremony). Next year will be our そつぎょうしき (graduation ceremony) and it will be us laughing, crying, signing autograph books and being presented to the principal to receive our そつぎょう しょうしょ (graduation certificate). I can't wait!

Have a think

1   Which events shown on these pages do you think are the most popular among students in Japan?
2   Which events do you think happen every year?
3   Which event would you like to experience, and why?

Have a go

1   Make a chart with the events shown here on one side and the events at your school on the other side.
2   Show which events are similar and which are different.
3   How can you explain the similarities and the differences?
4   Which event at your school do you think a Japanese student would most like to experience, and why?

ISBN 9780170196826

どうでしたか

うたいましょう

What I did on the weekend

This song is to the tune of 'Old MacDonald Had a Farm'.

Verse 1

しゅうまつに、 なにを、 しましたか。
しゅうまつに、 なにを、 しましたか。
えいがを　みました。
<ruby>テニス<rt>て に す</rt></ruby>を　しました。
えいが、 <ruby>テニス<rt>て に す</rt></ruby>、 えいが、 <ruby>テニス<rt>て に す</rt></ruby>
しゅうまつは、 ほんとうに、 たのしかった。

Verse 2

しゅうまつに、 なにを、 しましたか。
しゅうまつに、 なにを、 しましたか。
<ruby>スキー<rt>す き ー</rt></ruby>に　いきました。
すしを　たべました。
<ruby>スキー<rt>す き ー</rt></ruby>、 すし、 えいが、 <ruby>テニス<rt>て に す</rt></ruby>
しゅうまつは、 ほんとうに、 たのしかった。

Verse 3

しゅうまつに、 なにを、 しましたか。
しゅうまつに、 なにを、 しましたか。
iPodを　ききました。
ほんを　よみました。
iPod、 ほん、 <ruby>スキー<rt>す き ー</rt></ruby>、 すし、 えいが、 <ruby>テニス<rt>て に す</rt></ruby>
しゅうまつは、 ほんとうに、 たのしかった。
(Shout) つかれたー!!!

Corbis/amanaimages

ISBN 9780170196826

ごはんとおかず

ごはん

Alamy

Asking what someone did and responding

きのう、	なにを　しましたか。
Yesterday,	what did you do?
おこのみやきを　たべました。	
I ate okonomiyaki.	

Talking about what you did and did not do

休みに 金曜日の　ばん、	ケーキを　つくりました。 うみに　いきませんでした。
In the holidays, On Friday night,	I made a cake. I did not go to the beach.
休みに 金曜日の　ばん、	パーティーを　しましたか。 くつを　かいましたか。
In the holidays, On Friday night,	did you have a party? did you buy any shoes?
はい、　パーティーを　しましたか。 いいえ、　くつを　かいませんでし。	
Yes, I had a party. No, I did not buy any shoes.	

Asking what something was like and responding

りょこうは ローラーコースターは パーティーは	どう　でしたか。 こわかった　ですか。 たのしかった　ですか。
The holiday, The rollercoaster, The party,	what was it like? was it scary? was it fun?
たのしかった　です。 はい、　こわかった　です。 いいえ、　つまらなかった　です。	
It was fun. Yes, it was scary. No, it was boring.	

ISBN 9780170196826

12

二百十五

215

どうでしたか

おかず

12.3, 12.4

Time words

Core

きのう	yesterday
せんしゅう	last week
せんげつ	last month
きょねん	last year

Nouns

Core

としょかん	library
ローラーコースター	rollercoaster
さくぶん	composition
しけん	exam
じんじゃ	shrine
おてら	temple
りょこう	trip
おみやげ	souvenir

School events

More

にゅうがくしき	school entrance ceremony
ぶんかさい	cultural festival
うんどうかい	athletics carnival
キャンプ	school camp
なつ休み	summer holidays
すいえいたいかい	swimming carnival
しゅうがくりょこう	school trip
そつぎょうしき	graduation ceremony

The past form of adjectives

Core

うるさかった	was noisy
おいしかった	was delicious
おおきかった	was big
おかしかった	was funny; was strange
おもしろかった	was interesting; was funny
かわいかった	was cute
くさかった	was smelly
こわかった	was scary
すごかった	was amazing
たかかった	was expensive
たのしかった	was enjoyable
ちいさかった	was small
つまらなかった	was boring
まずかった	tasted awful
むずかしかった	was difficult
やさしかった	was easy
やすかった	was cheap
よかった	was good

Adjectives

Core

おいしい	delicious
おもしろい	interesting; funny
たかい	expensive
たのしい	fun
つまらない	boring
まずい	tastes awful
やさしい	easy
やすい	cheap

どうでしたか

ISBN 9780170196826

The past tense of verbs

Core

Verbs (past)		Verbs (past negative)	
たべました	I ate	たべませんでした	I did not eat
のみました	I drank	のみませんでした	I did not drink
みました	I saw; I watched	みませんでした	I did not see; I did not watch
ききました	I heard	ききませんでした	I did not hear
かきました	I wrote	かきませんでした	I did not write
よみました	I read	よみませんでした	I did not read
かいました	I bought	かいませんでした	I did not buy
とりました	I took	とりませんでした	I did not take
つくりました	I made	つくりませんでした	I did not make
しました	I did (do)	しませんでした	I did not (do)
いきました	I went	いきませんでした	I did not go
あいました	I met	あいませんでした	I did not meet
のりました	I caught; I took	のりませんでした	I did not catch; I did not take

iStockphoto

ISBN 9780170196826

どうでしたか

おしょうゆ

Here are some useful expressions from いただきます.

そう　でしたね。
That was right, wasn't it?
(past tense)

そうね。
That's right, isn't it?
(casual)

たいへん！
Oh no!

やきそば
fried noodles

しゃしんを　とって　ください。
Please take a photo.

カメラ（かめら）が　ありません。
I do not have my camera.

よかったね。
It was good, wasn't it?

まいこさん
geisha

それから
and then

まねきねこ
welcome cat
(a good-luck charm)

みせに　はいりました。
I went into the shops.
おみやげを　かいました。
I bought souvenirs.

Just think about all things you have learnt to say in Japanese and everything you have learnt about Japan. Thanks for sharing our stories! See you again in *Obento Supreme*!

おめでとう！

おめでとう！

おめでとう！

おめでとう！

SUMMER

KIYOMIZU TEMPLE

音羽山　清水寺

12

二百十八

218

どうでしたか

ISBN 9780170196826

せつめい

This section contains explanatory notes on the language taught in each unit.

Unit 1

Greeting and saying goodbye

a

When you address someone, you should use one of these titles after their name:
* さん Mr, Mrs or Ms
* くん (used after the first names of boys)
* ちゃん (used after the first names of children)
* せんせい teacher, doctor.

These words are used to show respect for the other person, so they are not used after your own name. When addressing your friends, you can use さん or くん. It is normal to use くん for boys and さん for girls, boys and anyone who is senior to you. You do not normally use さん when talking to young children.

You can use ちゃん instead of さん when talking to close friends or people in your family.

Girls often say ちゃん when talking to their friends at school. Boys tend to use くん.

People also often use ちゃん when talking to their pets.

b

When greeting someone by name, you generally say their name, then the greeting:
* エマさん、 こんにちは。
  Hello, Emma.
* せんせい、 おはようございます。
  Good morning, teacher.

Note how the comma is used after the person's name or title, in the same way as it is used in English.

c

Until about 11 a.m., おはようございます is used. This is because おはようございます used to mean 'it is early'. After about 11 a.m., you should say こんにちは。

d

After sunset you could say こんばんは, which means 'good evening'.

e

When greeting friends in the morning, you can say おはよう instead of おはようございます. In general, longer expressions in Japanese are more polite. You should not say おはよう to teachers or people who are senior to you.

f

Apart from さようなら, other (more casual) ways of saying goodbye include:
* また　あした。
  See you tomorrow.
* じゃ、　また。
  See you later.
* またね。
  See you!

Asking someone's name and introducing yourself

a

Two ways you can ask someone's name are:
* おなまえは？
  Your name is?
* おなまえは　なん　ですか。
  What is your name?

Note how なん　ですか can be replaced by a question mark.

b

Use these expressions to say who you are:
* わたしは　ケイト　です。
  I am Kate.
* ぼくは　ゆうすけ　です。
  I am Yuusuke.

c

It sounds like the 'u' at the end of です almost disappears! Usually, the 'u' sound is just said very faintly. In some parts of Japan, however, it is pronounced more strongly and you can hear it clearly.

ISBN 9780170196826

Giving instructions

a

Two common ways to give someone an instruction are:
- たって　ください。
  Please stand up.
  ちょっと　まって　ください。
  Just a minute, please.
- たって!
  Stand up!
  ちょっと　まって!
  Just a minute!

To ask someone politely to do something, you need to add ください, which is like saying 'please'. You should not omit ください when talking to your teacher or to people who are older than you. If you do not say ください, you will sound rude.

b

There are three ways you can tell someone to be quiet:
- しずかに!
  Quiet!
- しずかに　して!
  Be quiet!
- しずかに　して　ください。
  Please be quiet.

The longest expression is the most polite. Generally, to make your request less polite, leave off ください.

More

Three other commands are sometimes used in Japanese classrooms:
- きりつ!
  Stand!
- れい!
  Bow!
- ちゃくせき!
  Sit!

Here are a few more classroom expressions that your teacher may use:
- ノートに　かいて　ください。
  Please write it in your notebook.
- 日本ごで　いって　ください。
  Please say it in Japanese.
- えいごで　かいて　ください。
  Please write it in English.

You can be given more specific instructions if the teacher adds an object:
- ドアを　あけて　ください。
  Please open **the door**.
- ドアを　しめて　ください。
  Please close **the door**.

Note how the object is followed by を.

Unit 2

Counting to 20

a

Numbers can be written in Japanese in three ways:
- いち、に、さん
- 一、二、三
- 1、2、3

b

Numbers are generally only written in *kanji* when vertical writing is used, such as in newspapers or on business cards. At other times, Japanese numbers are written in digits as they are in English, but they are pronounced in Japanese.

c

Like many Japanese words, Japanese numbers originally came from Chinese. Some numbers, however, have kept their original Japanese pronunciation as well. These numbers can be pronounced in two different ways:
- 4,よん　し
- 7,なな　しち
- 9,きゅう　く

To many people, the number 4 is believed to be unlucky because its pronunciation sounds like the word that means 'death'. For this reason some hotels and hospitals do not have rooms with the number 4.

せつめい

ISBN 9780170196826

d

You can count large numbers by simply combining numbers:

- にじゅう 二十, 20
- にじゅういち 二十一, 21
- にじゅうご 二十五, 25
- さんじゅう 三十, 30
- さんじゅうさん 三十三, 33
- さんじゅうはち 三十八, 38
- よんじゅう 四十, 40
- よんじゅうろく 四十六, 46

- よんじゅうきゅう 四十九, 49
- きゅうじゅう 九十, 90
- きゅうじゅうに 九十二, 92
- きゅうじゅうなな 九十七, 97
- ひゃく 百, 100
- ひゃくじゅう 百十, 110
- ひゃくにじゅうご 百二十五, 125
- にひゃく 二百, 200

Asking someone's age and responding

a

To ask someone's age:
- なん さい ですか。
  What age are you?

When asking close friends how old they are, you can just ask:
- なんさい?
  How old?

b

To answer, replace the question word なん with a number, making sure to add さい. Note that some numbers change their pronunciation when they are used to give someone's age:
- 1 year old, いっさい
- 8 years old, はっさい
- 10 years old, じゅっさい
- 20 years old, はたち
  Use the same pattern for 11, 18 and 30.

However, for:
- 4 years old, use よんさい
- 7 years old, use ななさい
- 9 years old, use きゅうさい.

c

To ask another person, instead of repeating the questions, you can simply ask:
- ☐さんは?
  And what about ☐?
- ☐くんは?
  And what about ☐? (boy's name)

In Japanese, it is more polite to use a person's name than to say 'you'.

d

If you are the same age as someone else, you can say:
- わたしも じゅうさん 十三さい です。
  I am 13 years old too.

Asking someone's telephone number and responding

a

There are two ways to ask someone's telephone number:
- でんわ ばんごうは?
  Your telephone number, what is it?
- でんわ ばんごうは なん ですか。
  What is your telephone number?

b

When people say telephone numbers aloud, they usually say の after each group of numbers:
- 9236 4125 (written)
- 9236の4125 (spoken)

While this space between the numbers is pronounced の, it is not written as such; it is usually left as a space or indicated with a hyphen.

ISBN 9780170196826

せつめい

二百二十一

221

Unit 3

Asking where someone comes from and responding

a

In Japanese, the order of words in a sentence is different from English. For example, to ask where someone comes from and respond, you can say:

* どこ　から　きましたか。
  Where do you come from?
* オーストラリア　から　きました。
  I come from Australia.

Note that the question word どこ (where) is followed by から (from). The verb きました (I came) goes at the end. Also, note how in the answer the question word どこ can simply be replaced by the name of the country or the place.

b

Remember: you can easily recognise questions because they end in か.

Saying your nationality

To say your nationality, you say the name of the country you are from and add 人:

* わたしは　オーストラリア人　です。
  I am Australian.
* ぼくは　日本人　です。
  I am Japanese.

More

You can also use a simpler question and answer to ask where someone comes from and respond:

* どこ　から　ですか。
  Where are you from?
* オーストラリア　から　です。
  I am from Australia.

To be more specific about where you come from, you can say:

* オーストラリアの　アデレード　から　きました。
  I come from Adelaide, Australia.

Asking where someone lives and responding

To ask where someone lives, you can say:

* どこに　すんで　いますか。
  Where do you live?
  To answer, you can say:
* こうべに　すんで　います。
  I live in Kobe.

To answer, replace the question word どこ with the name of the place where you live. Note how the other words in the questions are repeated.

Unit 4

Asking how many people are in someone's family and responding

a

A common way to find out how many people are in someone's family is to ask:

* なん人　かぞく　ですか。
  How many people are in your family?

To answer, replace the question word なん with the number of people in the family:

* 五人　かぞく　です。
  There are five people in my family.
* 五人　です。
  There are five people.

b

In most cases, to count people, you simply say the number and add 人. However, some words for counting people have special pronunciations:

* 一人, 1 person
* 二人, 2 people
* 四人, 4 people

More

To say 'including me', you can say わたしを　いれて or ぼくを　いれて at the beginning of the sentence.

せつめい

ISBN 9780170196826

Saying who is in your family

a

To list all the people in your family, join the words with と, which means 'and', remembering to add yourself. At the end, say です。

- おとうさんと　おかあさんと　おばあさんと　わたし　です。
  Dad, Mum, Grandmother and me.

b

Some Japanese words have long vowel sounds. Be careful you do not skip these sounds or your speech will not sound truly Japanese.
Practise saying these words:

- おねえさん、　older sister
- おかあさん、　mother
- おにいさん、　older brother.

Asking someone if they have any pets and responding

a

A common way to find out if someone has any pets is to ask:

- ペットが　いますか。
  Do you have a pet?

  You can answer with:

- はい、　います。
  Yes, I do (have a pet).
- いいえ、　いません。
  No, I do not (have a pet).

b

If you want to say that you have more than one of a particular type of pet, the following expressions can be used:

- ねこが　二ひき　います。
  I have two cats.
- ねこが　三びきと　いぬが　二ひき　います。
  I have three cats and two dogs.

c

Similar expressions can be used to find out about someone's relatives:

- おじいさんが　いますか。
  Do you have a grandfather?
- いもうとが　いますか。
  Do you have a younger sister?

  You can answer with:

- はい、　います。
  Yes, I have.
- いいえ、　いません。
  No, I do not.

More

If you have more than one brother or sister, you can say:

- おねえさんが　二人　います。
  I have two sisters.
- おねえさんが　二人と　おとうとが　三人　います。
  I have two older sisters and three younger brothers.

  Do you notice the difference in the counting words used for people and animals?

Unit 5

Asking what someone's pet is and responding

a

When you want to find out what someone's pet is, you can ask:

- ペットは　なん　ですか。
  What is your pet? (What pet do you have?)

  To answer, replace the question word なん with the type of pet:

- ペットは　へび　です。
  (My) pet is a snake.

  Or more simply, you can say:

- いぬ　です。
  It is a dog.
- ねこ　です。
  It is a cat.

b

You could also give a long answer:

- わたしの／ぼくの　ペットは　うま　です。
  My pet is a horse.

  わたしの and ぼくの mean 'my'. Therefore, わたしの ペット means 'my pet'.

ISBN 9780170196826

二百二十三

せつめい

c

You can also talk about other people's pets:

- エマさんの　ペットは　へび　です。
  Emma's pet is a snake.

The の after a person's name is like an English apostrophe and 's':

- ハジョーノくんの　ペット
  Harjono's pet
- エマさんの　かぞく
  Emma's family.

d

A common way to tell someone a pet's name is to say:

- なまえは　ガーコ　です。
  Its name is Gaako.

Here are some other ways you can say someone's or something's name:

- ペットの　なまえは　ガーコ　です。
  My pet's name is Gaako.
- おねえさんの　なまえは　さゆり　です。
  My older sister's name is Sayuri.

More

To say 'my friend Ben', you can say:

- わたしの　ともだちの　ベン
  my friend Ben
- ともだちの　ベン
  (my) friend Ben.

Asking whose pet it is and describing pets

a

To find out whose pet it is, ask:

- だれの　ペット　ですか。
  Whose pet is it?

To answer, replace the question word だれ with the person's name:

- けんいちくんの　ペット　です。
  It is Kenichi's pet.

There is also a shorter answer:

- けんいちくんの　です。
  It is Kenichi's.

b

To describe something, use an adjective followed by です。

- うるさい　です。
  It is noisy.
- ちいさい　です。
  It is small.

You can be more specific by saying what you are describing, followed by は:

- あひるは　うるさい　です。
  The duck is / ducks are noisy.
- きんぎょは　ちいさい　です。
  The goldfish is / goldfish are small.

Asking what pets eat and drink and responding

a

There are two ways to ask what a pet eats:

- いぬは　なにを　たべますか。
  What does your dog eat?
- なにを　たべますか。
  What does it eat?

b

To answer, replace the question word なに with what the pet eats, followed by を and the verb たべます:

- にくを　たべます。
  It eats meat.
- いぬは　にくを　たべます。
  The dog eats meat.

c

You can say what you eat in the same way:

- わたしは　にくと　やさいを　たべます。
  I eat meat and vegetables.
- わたしは　パンを　たべます。
  I eat bread.

d

To ask what a pet drinks, say:

- ねこは　なにを　のみますか。
  What does your cat drink?

To answer, you can say:

- ねこは　みずを　のみます。
  It drinks water.

せつめい

ISBN 9780170196826

Unit 6

Asking about meals and responding

a

To ask someone what they eat and drink, say:

- なにを　たべますか。
  What do you eat?
- なにを　のみますか。
  What do you drink?

  You might also want to ask what someone eats for a particular meal:
- あさごはんに　なにを　たべますか。
  What do you eat for breakfast?
- ひるごはんに　なにを　たべますか。
  What do you eat for lunch?
- ばんごはんに　なにを　たべますか。
  What do you eat for dinner?

b

To answer, replace the question word なに with the name of a food:

- コーンフレークを　たべます。
  I eat cornflakes.
- サンドイッチを　たべます。
  I eat sandwiches.

Or:

- あさごはんに　コーンフレークを　たべます。
  I eat cornflakes for breakfast.
- ひるごはんに　サンドイッチを　たべます。
  I eat sandwiches for lunch.

More

When talking about what people drink at breakfast, it sounds strange in Japanese to say あさごはんに なにを のみますか. You should therefore say:

- あさごはん**の ときに** なにを　のみますか。
  At breakfast time what do you drink?

  Or simply (when the meal you are talking about has already been stated):
- なにを　のみますか。
  What do you drink?

  You could then answer:
- ミルクを　のみます。
  I drink milk.

Talking about likes and dislikes

a

The most common way to ask if someone likes something is to ask:

- すき　ですか。
  Do you like it?

  You can be more specific:
- パスタが　すき　ですか。
  Do you like pasta?
- ソーセージが　すき　ですか。
  Do you like sausages?

b

There are several ways to answer when someone asks if you like something:

- はい、　すき　です。
  Yes, I like it.
- はい、　だいすき　です。
  Yes, I like it a lot.
- いいえ、　あんまり...
  No, not very much.
- いいえ、　きらい　です。
  No, I do not like it.
- いいえ、　だいきらい　です。
  No, I hate it. (Be careful using this. It can sound rude.)

c

You can ask if someone eats or drinks something:

- コーンフレークを　たべますか。
  Do you eat cornflakes?
- コーヒーを　のみますか。
  Do you drink coffee?

d

You can answer 'yes' or 'no':

- はい、　たべます。
  Yes, I eat it.
- はい、　のみます。
  Yes, I drink it.
- いいえ、　たべません。
  No, I do not eat it.
- いいえ、　のみません。
  No, I do not drink it.

二百二十五

225

せつめい

ISBN 9780170196826

More

To be polite, when people do not like something, they mostly say いいえ、 あんまり... If answering with a complete sentence, say:

- いいえ、 あまり すき じゃない です。
  No, I do not like it very much.

  When you want to mention how often you eat or drink something, you can say:
- まいにち たべます。
  I eat it every day.
- まいにち のみます。
  I drink it every day.
- よく たべます。
  I eat it often.
- よく のみます。
  I drink it often.
- ときどき たべます。
  I eat it sometimes.
- ときどき のみます。
  I drink it sometimes.
- ぜんぜん たべません。
  I do not eat it at all.
- ぜんぜん のみ**ません**。
  I do not drink it at all.

  Note how ます changes to ません when using ぜんぜん.

  You could also say that you do not eat or drink something very much:
- いいえ、 あまり たべ**ません**。
  No, I do not eat it very much.
- いいえ、 あまり のみ**ません**。
  No, I do not drink it very much.

  Note how ます changes to ません when using あまり.

Unit 7

Asking the day and responding

To find out what day of the week it is, you can ask:

- なん曜日 ですか。
  What day of the week is it?
- きょうは なん曜日 ですか。
  What day of the week is today?

To answer, replace なん with the day of the week.

- 月曜日 です。
  It is Monday.
- きょうは 月曜日 です。
  Today is Monday.

Asking the date and responding

To find out what date it is, you can ask:

- なん月 なん日 ですか。
  What is the date?
- きょうは なん月 なん日 ですか。
  What is the date today?

To answer, replace なん with the month and date.

- 七月 十四日 です。
  It is 14 July.
- きょうは 七月 十四日 です。
  Today is 14 July.

Asking when an event will take place and responding

a

To find out when something takes place, the most common way is to ask:

- たんじょうびは いつ ですか。
  When is your birthday?
- キャンプは いつ ですか。
  When is the camp?

b

To answer, replace the question word いつ with the date or day:

- 8月30日 です。
  It is 30 August.
- 金曜日 です。
  It is Friday.

せつめい

ISBN 9780170196826

c

Another way is to ask what date or what day:

- たんじょうびは　なん月　なん日　ですか。
  What date is your birthday?
- キャンプは　なん曜日　ですか。
  What day is the camp?

More

To find out when the holidays are, you need to use the words から (from) and まで (until). Then you can ask:

- 休みは　いつ　から　ですか。
  From when are the holidays?

- 休みは　いつ　まで　ですか。
  Until when are the holidays?
- 休みは　いつ　から　いつ　まで　ですか。
  From when and until when are the holidays?
  Or you can use なん月　なん日 to be more specific:
- 休みは　なん月　なん日　から　ですか。
  From what date are the holidays?

Note that the Japanese school holidays are named according to the season they are in, for example, なつ休み (summer holidays).

Unit 8

Asking about hobbies and interests and responding

a

To find out what someone's hobbies or interests are, you can ask:

- しゅみは　なん　ですか。
  What is your hobby/interest?

You can use a person's name and ask:

- ゆうすけくんの　しゅみは　なん　ですか。
  What is Yuusuke's hobby/interest?

b

To answer, replace the question word なん with the hobby or interest:

- スポーツ　です。
  It is sport.
- どくしょと　ピアノ　です。
  They are reading books and (playing) the piano.

Or you can answer using longer sentences:

- しゅみは　スポーツ　です。
  (My) hobby is sport.
- わたしの　しゅみは　スポーツ　です。
  My hobby is sport.

Asking about sports and responding

a

To find out what kind of sports someone plays, you can ask:

- どんな　スポーツを　しますか。
  What kind of sports do you play?

To answer, use the name of the sport followed by the particle を and します:

- バスケットボールを　します。
  I play basketball.
- すいえいと　テニスを　します。
  I swim and play tennis.

b

You can also ask if someone plays sport generally or one sport in particular:

- スポーツを　しますか。
  Do you play sport?
- からてを　しますか。
  Do you do karate?

Note that します can mean 'to do' or 'to play'. There are two ways you can answer:

- はい、　します。
  Yes, I do.
- いいえ、　しません。
  No, I do not.

c

To ask what kind of sports, food or music someone likes, say:

- どんな　スポーツが　すき　ですか。
  What sports do you like?
- どんな　りょうりが　すき　ですか。
  What food do you like?
- どんな　おんがくが　すき　ですか。
  What music do you like?

ISBN 9780170196826

せつめい

Talking about what someone can do

a

To find out if someone can do something, you can ask:

- からてが　できますか。
  Can you do karate?
- インドネシアご_{いんどねしあ}が　できますか。
  Can you do (speak) Indonesian?

Note how the particle が is used with できます.

b

There are different ways you can answer:

- はい、　できます。
  Yes, I can.
- いいえ、　できません。
  No, I cannot.

By adding other words, you can say how well you can (or cannot) do something:

- はい、　すこし　できます。
  Yes, I can a little.
- いいえ、　あまり　できません。
  No, I cannot do it very well.
- いいえ、　ぜんぜん　できません。
  No, I cannot at all.

c

To say what you can or cannot do, say the activity followed by が and できます or できません.

- じょうばが　できます。
  I can do horse riding. (I can ride horses.)
- りょうりが　できません。
  I cannot do cooking. (I cannot cook.)
- けんどうが　あまり　できません。
  I cannot do kendo very well.

Unit 9

Asking where someone is going on the weekend and responding

a

To find out where someone is going, you can ask:

- どこに　いきますか。
  Where are you going?

To answer, add the particle に and the verb いきます to the place:

- うみに　いきます。
  I am going to the beach.

b

To say whose house you are going to or which game you are going to watch, you need to use the particle の:

- エマさんの　うちに　いきます。
  I am going to Emma's house.
- テニスの　しあいに　いきます。
  I am going to watch a tennis match.

c

To say you are not going somewhere, use the verb ending ません.

- がっこうに　いきますか。
  Are you going to school?
- がっこうに　いきません。
  I am not going to school.

d

The phrase 'on the weekend' is しゅうまつに in Japanese. You can also add the particle に to some other time words and expressions:

- 日曜日_{にちようび}に、　on Sunday
- 十五日_{じゅうごにち}に、　on the 15th
- 三月_{さんがつ}に、　　in March.

Asking who someone is going with and responding

a

To find out who someone is going with, you can ask:

- だれと　いきますか。
  Who are you going with?

b

If you are going by yourself, you can say:

- 一人_{ひとり}で　いきます。
  I am going by myself.

c

Or, replace the question word だれ with the person's name:

- ゆきさんと　いきます。
  I am going with Yuki.
- ゆきさんと　うみに　いきます。
  I am going to the beach with Yuki.

せつめい

ISBN 9780170196826

Asking how someone is getting there and responding

a

To find out how someone is going somewhere, you can ask:

- なんで　いきますか。
  By what means are you going?
  (How are you going?)

  Note how the particle で is used with なん.
  Another way is to use the question word どう　やって:

- どう　やって　いきますか。
  How are you going there?

b

If you want to say by what means of transport you are going, you can replace the question word なん with the type of transport.

- バ<ruby>ス<rt>す</rt></ruby>で　いきます。
  I am going by bus.
- くるまで　いきます。
  I am going by car.

c

To say that you walked, you can say:

- あるいて　いきます。
  I am going on foot.

Unit 10

Asking about daily activities and responding

a

To find out what someone is going to do, you can ask:

- なにを　しますか。
  What will you do? / What do you do? / What will you be doing?

  You might want to ask what they are going to do on a particular day. Many words indicating specific times are followed by the particle に.

- <ruby>土曜日<rt>どようび</rt></ruby>に　なにを　しますか。
  What will you be doing on Saturday?
- しゅうまつに　なにを　しますか。
  What will you be doing on the weekend?

  However, many other more general time words do not take the particle に.

- きょう　なにを　しますか。
  What will you be doing today?
- あした　なにを　しますか。
  What will you be doing tomorrow?

b

To answer, say what you are going to do:

- <ruby>テレビ<rt>てれび</rt></ruby>を　みます。
  I am going to watch television.
- おんがくを　ききます。
  I am going to listen to music.

c

You have seen the particle を in questions such as:

- なにを　たべますか。
  What do you eat?
- なにを　のみますか。
  What do you drink?
- なにを　しますか。
  What do/will you do?

  And in statements such as:

- <ruby>サンドイッチ<rt>さんどいっち</rt></ruby>を　たべます。
  I eat sandwiches.
- <ruby>ミルク<rt>みるく</rt></ruby>を　のみます。
  I drink milk.

  The particle を tells you what the object of the sentence is and is placed after the object. The object of a sentence is the person or thing having the action done to it (i.e. what you eat, drink or do).

Talking about daily activities you do or do not do

a

To say you do something, use the verb ending ます.

- よみます。
  I read.
- <ruby>本<rt>ほん</rt></ruby>を　よみます。
  I read books.

b

To say you do not do something, use the verb ending ません.

- よみません。
  I do not read.
- <ruby>本<rt>ほん</rt></ruby>を　よみません。
  I do not read books.

ISBN 9780170196826

二百二十九

せつめい

Unit 11

Asking about free time and responding

a

When talking about free time, you can use:
- がっこうの　あと, after school
- がっこうの　まえに, before school
- ひまな　ときに, in (your/my) free time
- 金曜日の　ばん, on Friday nights
- あしたの　あさ, tomorrow morning
- あしたの　ばん, tomorrow night
- あさ, in the morning
- よる, in the evening

Note how some expressions take the particle で, some take the particle に and others need no particle at all.

b

To ask what someone does at a particular time, add なにを　しますか to the time phrase:
- ひまな　ときに　なにを　しますか。
  What do you do in your free time?
- がっこうの　あとで　なにを　しますか。
  What do you do after school?

c

To answer, you will need to use an object followed by を and a verb ending in ます:
- パーティーを　します。
  I have parties.
- テレビを　みます。
  I watch television.
- てがみを　かきます。
  I write letters.

  Note:
- ともだちに　でんわを　します。
  I phone my friend.
- ともだちに　あいます。
  I meet my friend.
- ねます。
  I sleep.

More

You can talk about other things you **also** do by changing を to も:
- ほんも　よみます。
  I also read books.
- えいがも　みます。
  I also watch movies.
- おんがくも　ききます。
  I also listen to music.

Suggesting something and responding

To suggest doing something with someone, you can use the verb ending ましょう:
- アイスクリームを　たべましょう。
  Let's eat ice-cream.
- えいがを　みましょう。
  Let's see a movie.

  If you agree with the suggestion, you can say:
- はい、　みましょう。
  Let's see it.

- はい、　いっしょに　みましょう。
  Let's see it together.
- はい、　そう　しましょう。
  Yes, let's do so.

  If you do not agree with the suggestion, you can say:
- いいえ、　それは　ちょっと...
  No, that's not so good.

Expressing opinions and responding

a

To say what you think about something, use です after an adjective.
- たのしい　です。
  It is fun.
- おいしい　です。
  It is delicious.
- 日本ごは　むずかしい　です。
  Japanese is difficult.

b

If you want the other person to give their opinion in response to yours, add ね:
- たのしい　ですね。
  It is fun, isn't it?
- おいしい　ですね。
  It is delicious, isn't it?
- そう　ですね。
  It is, isn't it?

二百三十

せつめい

ISBN 9780170196826

c

You can agree or disagree by expressing your opinion more strongly. To do this, add よ:

- たのしい　ですよ。
  It is fun, I tell you.

- おいしい　ですよ。
  It is delicious, you know.

- そう　ですよ。
  It sure is!

Unit 12

Asking what someone did and responding

a

When asking what someone did, you can say:

- 火曜日に　なにを　しましたか。
  <ruby>火曜日<rt>かようび</rt></ruby>
  What did you do on Tuesday?

b

In the past tense, verbs end in ました. Verbs that require an object take を:

- えいがを　みました。
  I watched a movie.

Verbs that describe moving towards or away from something – such as meeting someone, catching something and going somewhere – take に:

- しあいに　いきました。
  I went to the game.

- ベンくんに　あいました。
  I met Ben.

c

To continue and talk about something else you did, begin the second sentence with そして:

- そして、　ざっしを　かいました。
  And I bought a magazine.

Talking about what you did and did not do

a

To say that you did not do something, change the verb ending from ました to ませんでした:

- えいがに　いきませんでした。
  I did not go to the movies.

b

Here are examples of how you could ask someone what they did at a certain time:

- 4月13日に　なにを　しましたか。
  What did you do on 13 April?

- きのう、　なにを　しましたか。
  What did you do yesterday?

- がっこうの　あとで　なにを　しました。
  What did you do after school?

- 休みに　なにを　しましたか。
  What did you do during the holidays?

Specific points in time, such as '13 April', are followed by に. General points in time, such as 'yesterday', are followed by a comma. Note how the expressions がっこうの　あと (after school) and 休みに (in the holidays) can also be used.

c

Note the expression:

- おかあさんに　てがみを　かきました。
  I wrote a letter to my mother.

d

To say that you did something for the first time, use はじめて:

- はじめて　さしみを　たべました。
  I ate raw fish for the first time.

Asking what something was like and responding

a

To find out what something was like, you can ask:

- どう　でしたか。
  What was it like?

b

To answer, change the い on the end of the adjective to かった and add です:

- おいしかった　です。
  It was delicious.

- たのしかった　です。
  It was fun.

c

You can also begin a sentence with 'but' when adding another sentence:

- でも、　えいがは　つまらなかった　です。
  But the movie was boring.

- でも、　すしは　まずかった　です。
  But the sushi was awful.

ISBN 9780170196826

せつめい

Tables

Exclamations and interjections

Oohs and aahs

Oh! Ah!	あ！ ああ！ あー！ あっ！
Oh?	あれ？ あれっ？
Uhh?	んん？
Mmm	うーん
Um	えーと
Hey!	あのー！ あのねー！ ねえ！
Right. Well. Okay.	じゃ じゃあ
Huh! Hey! What! Eh!	え！ ええ！ えー！ えっ！
What?	なぁに？ なに？
Now	さあ

Is that so?

You're kidding! You're lying!	うそ！ うそー！
Just as I thought!	やっぱり！
Is that right? Is that so? Really?	そう？ そーう？ そう ですか。(polite)
That's right!	そう です。 そう ですよ。 そうね！ (girls) そうだよ！ (boys)
That's right, isn't it?	そう ですね。 そうね。 そう でしたね。(past tense)

Bad news!

That's awful!	いやだ！ やだ！ やだー！
Aagh! Ah! (screaming)	きゃー！
Bad luck! That's a pity!	ざんねん です！ ざんねん ですね。
No good! No!	だめ！
Oh no!	たいへん！
That's disgusting!	ひどーい！
Late!	おそーい！

Really?

That's unbelievable! I can't believe it!	しんじられない！
Really? Truly?	ほんとう？ ほんとうに？
Really?	へえ？ へー？ へえー？ へええー？
That's not right	ちがいます

Yes and no

Yeah! Yes!	うん！ はい！ はーい！
Okay!	いいよ！
Let's do that!	そう しましょう！
No!	ううん！ いいえ

Good news!

Okay! All right!	だいじょうぶ！ だいじょうぶよ！
That's great, isn't it?	いい ですね。 いいね！
Wow!	わあ！ ワー！ わー！
Well done! Good!	よし！
Wow! Incredible! Amazing!	すごい！ すごーい！
Great! I am so happy!	うれしい！
Cool! Wonderful!	すてき！
It was good, wasn't it?	よかったね。
Yay! I've done it!	やったー！ わーい！
Looking forward to it!	たのしみ！

Good effort!

Push! Heave!	よいしょ！
I'm so tired!	つかれたー！
Here you are!	どうぞ！

ISBN 9780170196826

Adjectives

Present		Past	
いい	good	よかった	was good
うるさい	noisy	うるさかった	was noisy
うれしい	happy	うれしかった	was happy
おいしい	delicious	おいしかった	was delicious
おおきい	big	おおきかった	was big
おかしい	funny; strange	おかしかった	was funny; was strange
おもしろい	interesting; funny	おもしろかった	was interesting; was funny
かわいい	cute	かわいかった	was cute
くさい	smelly	くさかった	was smelly
こわい	scary	こわかった	was scary
すごい	amazing	すごかった	was amazing
たかい	expensive	たかかった	was expensive
たのしい	fun	たのしかった	was enjoyable
ちいさい	small	ちいさかった	was small
つまらない	boring	つまらなかった	was boring
まずい	tastes awful	まずかった	tasted awful
むずかしい	difficult	むずかしかった	was difficult
やさしい	easy	やさしかった	was easy
やすい	cheap	やすかった	was cheap

おいしい

かわいい

うるさい

おおきい

Photos by Alamy, Corbis/Haruyoshi Yamaguchi, Ioan Liviu-Orletchi, Shutterstock.com/J Henning Buchholz

二百三十三

ISBN 9780170196826

Verbs

Present		Negative		Past	
あいます	meet	あいません	do not meet	あいました	met
あけます	open	あけません	do not open	あけました	opened
あります	have	ありません	do not have	ありました	had
いいます	say	いいません	do not say	いいました	said
いきます	go	いきません	do not go	いきました	went
います	have; exist	いません	do not have; do not exist	いました	had; existed
いれます	put it in; let it in	いれません	do not put it in	いれました	put it in
うたいます	sing	うたいません	do not sing	うたいました	sang
おわります	finish; end	おわりません	do not finish	おわりました	finished
かいます	buy	かいません	do not buy	かいました	bought
かえります	return; go back (home)	かえりません	do not return	かえりました	returned
かきます	write	かきません	do not write	かきました	wrote
かします	lend	かしません	do not lend	かしました	lent
かぞえます	count	かぞえません	do not count	かぞえました	counted
かちます	win	かちません	do not win	かちました	won
ききます	listen	ききません	do not listen	ききました	heard
きます	come	きません	do not come	きました	came
します	do; play; hold (e.g. hold a party)	しません	do not do; do not play; do not hold	しました	I did (do)
しめます	shut; close	しめません	do not shut	しめました	shut
しって います	know	しりません	do not know		
すわります	sit; sit down	すわりません	do not sit	すわりました	sat
すんで います	live	すんで いません	do not live	すんで いました	lived

ISBN 9780170196826

Past negative		Let's		Please	
あいません でした	did not meet	あいましょう	let's meet	あって ください	please meet
あけません でした	did not open	あけましょう	let's open	あけて ください	please open
ありません でした	did not have				
いいません でした	did not say	いいましょう	let's say	いって ください	please say
いきません でした	did not go	いきましょう	let's go	いって ください	please go
いません でした	was not				
いれません でした	did not put it in	いれましょう	let's put it in	いれて ください	please put it in
うたいません でした	did not sing	うたいましょう	let's sing	うたって ください	please sing
おわりません でした	did not finish	おわりましょう	let's finish	おわって ください	please finish
かいません でした	did not buy	かいましょう	let's buy	かって ください	please buy
かえりません でした	did not return	かえりましょう	let's go back	かえて ください	please return
かきません でした	did not write	かきましょう	let's write	かいて ください	please write
かしません でした	did not lend	かしましょう	let's lend	かして ください	please lend
かぞえません でした	did not count	かぞえましょう	let's count	かぞえて ください	please count
かちません でした	did not win	かちましょう	let's win	かって ください	please win
ききません でした	did not hear	ききましょう	let's listen	きいて ください	please listen
きません でした	did not come	きましょう	let's come	きて ください	please come
しません でした	I did not (do)	しましょう	let's do; let's play	して ください	please do
しめません でした	did not shut	しめましょう	let's shut	しめて ください	please shut
しりません でした	did not know				
すわりません でした	did not sit	すわりましょう	let's sit	すわって ください	please sit
すんで いません でした	did not live				

ISBN 9780170196826

Present		Negative		Past	
だします	take out	だしません	do not take out	だしました	took out
たちます	stand	たちません	do not stand	たちました	stood
たべます	eat	たべません	do not eat	たべました	ate
ちがいます	is different	ちがいません	is not different	ちがいました	was different
つくります	make	つくりません	do not make	つくりました	made
できます	can do	できません	cannot do	できました	could do
です	be; is	じゃない　です	is not	でした	was
とります	take; record	とりません	do not take; do not record	とりました	took
ねます	sleep	ねません	do not sleep	ねました	slept
のこします	leave behind	のこしません	do not leave behind	のこしました	left behind
のせます	put on top	のせません	do not put on top	のせました	put on top
のみます	drink	のみません	do not drink	のみました	drank
のります	catch; take; ride; get on	のりません	do not ride; do not get on	のりました	rode; got on
はいります	enter; come in	はいりません	do not enter	はいりました	entered
はなします	talk; speak; say	はなしません	do not talk; do not speak	はなしました	spoke; talked
ひっくり かえします	turn over	ひっくり かえしません	do not turn over	ひっくり かえしました	turned over
まぜます	mix	まぜません	do not mix	まぜました	mixed
まちます	wait	まちません	do not wait	まちました	waited
みせます	show	みせません	do not show	みせました	showed
みます	watch; look at	みません	do not watch; do not look at	みました	watched; looked at
やきます	grill; fry	やきません	do not grill; do not fry	やきました	grilled; fried
よみます	read	よみません	do not read	よみました	read
わかります	understand	わかりません	do not understand	わかりました	understood

ISBN 9780170196826

Past negative		Let's		Please	
だしません でした	did not take out	だしましょう	let's take out	だして ください	please take out
たちません でした	did not stand	たちましょう	let's stand	たって ください	please stand
たべません でした	did not eat	たべましょう	let's eat	たべて ください	please eat
ちがいません でした	was not different				
つくりません でした	did not make	つくりましょう	let's make	つくって ください	please make
できません でした	could not do				
じゃなかった です	was not				
とりません でした	did not take	とりましょう	let's take	とって ください	please take
ねません でした	did not sleep	ねましょう	let's sleep	ねて ください	please sleep
のこしません でした	did not leave behind	のこしましょう	let's leave behind	のこして ください	please leave it
のせません でした	did not put on top	のせましょう	let's put on top	のせて ください	please put on top
のみません でした	did not drink	のみましょう	let's drink	のんで ください	please drink
のりません でした	did not ride; did not get on	のりましょう	let's ride; let's get on	のって ください	please ride; please get on
はいりません でした	did not enter	はいりましょう	let's enter	はいって ください	please enter
はなしません でした	did not talk; did not speak	はなしましょう	let's talk; let's speak	はなして ください	please talk; please speak
ひっくり かえしません でした	did not turn over	ひっくり かえしましょう	let's turn over	ひっくり かえして ください	please turn over
まぜません でした	did not mix	まぜましょう	let's mix	まぜて ください	please mix
まちません	did not wait	まちましょう	let's wait	まって ください	please wait
みせません でした	did not show	みせましょう	let's show	みせて ください	please show
みません でした	did not watch; did not look at	みましょう	let's watch; let's look at	みて ください	please watch; please look at
やきません でした	did not grill; did not fry	やきましょう	let's grill; let's fry	やいて ください	please grill; please fry
よみません でした	did not read	よみましょう	let's read	よんで ください	please read
わかりません でした	did not understand			わかって ください	please understand

二百三十七

Particles

は		
subject marker	わたし**は** たかこ です。	I am Takako.
も		
also; too	ぼく**も** 十二^{じゅうに}さい です。	I am also 12 years old.
か		
question marker	どこ から きました**か**。	Where do you come from?
から		
from	日本^{にほん} **から** きました。	I come from Japan.
が		
used with います	ねこ**が** います。	I have a cat.
used with すき and きらい	くだもの**が** すき です。	I like fruit.
used with できます	りょうり**が** できます。	I can cook.
と		
and	ゆきさん**と** けんいちくん です。	It is Yuki and Kenichi.
with	おかあさん**と** いきます。	I am going with mum.
の		
possession marker	わたし**の** いぬ です。	It is my dog.
of	テニス^{てにす}**の** しあいに いきます。	I am going to a game of tennis.
を		
object marker	にく**を** たべます。	I eat meat.
に		
for	あさごはん**に** なにを たべますか。	What do you eat for breakfast?
on	日曜日^{にちようび}**に** しあいに いきます。	I am going to the game on Sunday.
	えいが**に** いきます。	I am going to a movie.
to	ともだち**に** でんわを します。	I am going to phone (to) my friend.
used with あいます	せんせい**に** あいました。	I met a teacher.
used with のります	でんしゃ**に** のりました。	I rode on a train.
で		
in	日本^{にほん}ご**で** かきます。	I will write it in Japanese.
by	バス^{ばす}**で** いきました。	I went by bus.
	みんな**で** たべましょう。	Let's eat all together (with everyone).
	一人^{ひとり}**で** いきます。	I am going alone.
	ぜんぶ**で** 六人^{ろくにん} です。	There are six people in all.
used in expressions	あと**で**、 えいがを みましょう。	Let's watch a movie later.
ね		
isn't it? wasn't it?	いい です**ね**。	That is good, isn't it?
よ		
used to emphasise	おもしろい です**よ**。	It is interesting, you know!

ISBN 9780170196826

Numbers

0	れい or ゼロ	〇
1	いち	一
2	に	二
3	さん	三
4	し or よん	四
5	ご	五
6	ろく	六
7	しち or なな	七
8	はち	八
9	きゅう or く	九
10	じゅう	十
11	じゅういち	十一
12	じゅうに	十二
13	じゅうさん	十三
14	じゅうし or じゅうよん	十四
15	じゅうご	十五
16	じゅうろく	十六
17	じゅうしち or じゅうなな	十七
18	じゅうはち	十八
19	じゅうきゅう or じゅうく	十九
20	にじゅう	二十
21	にじゅういち	二十一
22	にじゅうに	二十二
30	さんじゅう	三十
31	さんじゅういち	三十一
40	よんじゅう	四十
50	ごじゅう	五十
60	ろくじゅう	六十
70	ななじゅう	七十
80	はちじゅう	八十
90	きゅうじゅう	九十
99	きゅうじゅうきゅう	九十九
100	ひゃく	百

Ages

1 year old	いっさい	一さい
2 years old	にさい	二さい
3 years old	さんさい	三さい
4 years old	よんさい	四さい
5 years old	ごさい	五さい
6 years old	ろくさい	六さい
7 years old	ななさい	七さい
8 years old	はっさい	八さい
9 years old	きゅうさい	九さい
10 years old	じゅっさい	十さい
11 years old	じゅういっさい	十一さい
12 years old	じゅうにさい	十二さい
13 years old	じゅうさんさい	十三さい
14 years old	じゅうよんさい	十四さい
15 years old	じゅうごさい	十五さい
16 years old	じゅうろくさい	十六さい
17 years old	じゅうななさい	十七さい
18 years old	じゅうはっさい	十八さい
19 years old	じゅうきゅうさい	十九さい
20 years old	はたち	二十

Number of people

1 person	ひとり	一人
2 people	ふたり	二人
3 people	さんにん	三人
4 people	よにん	四人
5 people	ごにん	五人
6 people	ろくにん	六人
7 people	しちにん	七人
8 people	はちにん	八人
9 people	きゅうにん	九人
10 people	じゅうにん	十人

ISBN 9780170196826

Days of the week

にちようび	日曜日	Sunday
げつようび	月曜日	Monday
かようび	火曜日	Tuesday
すいようび	水曜日	Wednesday
もくようび	木曜日	Thursday
きんようび	金曜日	Friday
どようび	土曜日	Saturday

Dates

ついたち	一日	1st
ふつか	二日	2nd
みっか	三日	3rd
よっか	四日	4th
いつか	五日	5th
むいか	六日	6th
なのか	七日	7th
ようか	八日	8th
ここのか	九日	9th
とおか	十日	10th
じゅういちにち	十一日	11th
じゅうににち	十二日	12th
じゅうさんにち	十三日	13th
じゅうよっか	十四日	14th
じゅうごにち	十五日	15th
じゅうろくにち	十六日	16th
じゅうしちにち	十七日	17th
じゅうはちにち	十八日	18th
じゅうくにち	十九日	19th
はつか	二十日	20th
にじゅういちにち	二十一日	21st
にじゅうににち	二十二日	22nd
にじゅうさんにち	二十三日	23rd
にじゅうよっか	二十四日	24th
にじゅうごにち	二十五日	25th
にじゅうろくにち	二十六日	26th
にじゅうしちにち	二十七日	27th
にじゅうはちにち	二十八日	28th
にじゅうくにち	二十九日	29th
さんじゅうにち	三十日	30th
さんじゅういちにち	三十一日	31st

Months

いちがつ	一月	January
にがつ	二月	February
さんがつ	三月	March
しがつ	四月	April
ごがつ	五月	May
ろくがつ	六月	June
しちがつ	七月	July
はちがつ	八月	August
くがつ	九月	September
じゅうがつ	十月	October
じゅういちがつ	十一月	November
じゅうにがつ	十二月	December

Corbis/Bloomimage

わたしの　たんじょうびは　十月 三日　です。

Tables

ISBN 9780170196826

Glossary

にほん
日本ご～えいご
Japanese-English

あ	English	Unit
アーチェリー	archery	11
あいきどう	aikido	8
アイスクリーム	ice-cream	6
アイデア	idea	11
アイポッド	iPod	10
あいます	meet	10
あお	blue	12
あおのり	seaweed flakes	6
あか	red	12
アカウント	account	10
あかちゃん	baby	4
あきまつり	Autumn Festival	7
あけて（ください）	open it (please)	1
あさ	morning	11
あさごはん	breakfast	6
あじ	flavour	1
あした	tomorrow	7
アップルジュース	apple juice	1
アップロード	upload	11
アデレード	Adelaide	3
あと；あとで	later; after; afterwards	9
あなた	you	6
あなたの	your	8
アニメ	animated movie	10
あひる	duck	4
アプリ	application	10
アプリケーション	application	10
あまり	not much; not really; not well	6
あみだくじ	Japanese ladder puzzle	5
アメリカ	America; United States of America	3
あられ	rice crackers	7
ありがとう	thanks; thank you	1
ありがとうございました	thank you very much	2

ありがとうございます	thank you	1
あります	have	12
あるいて	on foot	9
あれ	that (one over there)	2
アンケート	survey	4
あんまり	not much; not really; not well	6
あんみつ	a type of Japanese sweet	6

い	English	Unit
いい	good	5
いいえ	no	1
イースター	Easter	7
イーブック	ebook	10
いきます	go	5
いけばな	flower arranging	8
いそがしい	busy	10
いただきます	thanks before a meal	1
イタリア	Italy	3
一	one	2
一月	January	7
一がっき	one semester	12
一だん	level 1	3
いちど	once	4
一日	one day	1
一ねん	one year	7
一ねんせい	first-year students	12
いつ	when	7
五日	5th day of the month	7
一さい	1 year old	2
いっしょに	together	11
いって（ください）	say (please)	1
いつも	always	8
いぬ	dog	4
イベント	event	11

ISBN 9780170196826

二百四十一

いま	now	8
います	have; is; be	4
いもうと	younger sister	4
いもうとさん	younger sister (someone else's)	4
いらっしゃい	welcome; come in	10
いれます	put in	6
インターネット	Internet	10
インタビュー	interview	11
インドネシア	Indonesia	3

う	English	Unit
ウィークエンド	weekend	9
ウィキペディア	Wikipedia	10
ウェブ	web	10
ウェブサイト	website	10
ウェブデザイン	web design	10
うさぎ	rabbit	4
うそ	lie	5
うたいます	sing	1
うち	house; home	9
うどん	noodles	1
うなぎ	eel	6
うま	horse	4
うみ	beach; ocean	9
うめぼし	pickled plums	6
うるさい	noisy	5
うれしい	happy	2
うわばき	indoor shoes; slippers	1
うんどうかい	sports carnival; athletics carnival	7

え	English	Unit
えいが	movie; movies	9
えいがかん	cinema	12
えいご	English language	8
ええ	yes	9
エクストラ	extra	10
えさ	pet food; animal food	5
えび	prawns	6
エミュー	emu	11

円	yen (Japanese currency)	1
えんげき（ぶ）	drama (club)	10
えんそく	excursion	6

お	English	Unit
おいしい	delicious	5
おうえん	cheer	12
おおきい	big; large	5
オークランド	Auckland	3
オーストラリア	Australia	3
オーストラリアン フットボール	Australian rules football	8
おかあさん	mother; mum	4
おかし	sweets	1
おかしい	funny; strange	5
おかず	side dishes	1
おげんき　ですか	how are you?	10
おこのみに	as you like; according to taste	6
おこのみやき	Japanese-style savoury pancake	6
おじいさん	grandfather; old man	4
おしいれ	cupboard for futon	1
おしまい	the end	5
おしょうがつ	New Year	7
おしょうゆ	soya sauce	1
おせちりょうり	New Year's food	12
おそい	late	9
おそく　なって すみません	sorry, I am late	9
おたく	geek	11
おたんじょうび	birthday	2
おたんじょうび おめでとう	happy birthday	2
おちゃ	green tea	1
おつかれさま	thank you for your hard work	8
おてら	temple (Buddhist)	12
おとうさん	father	4
おとうと	younger brother	4
おとうとさん	younger brother (someone else's)	4
おなまえ	name	1
おに	ogre; devil	5
おにいさん	older brother	4
おにぎり	rice balls	1

ISBN 9780170196826

おにども	ogres	5
おねえさん	older sister	4
おねがい	request	2
おばあさん	grandmother; old woman	4
おばけやしき	haunted house	12
おばさん	aunt	9
おはし	chopsticks	1
おはよう	good morning (*casual*)	1
おはようございます	good morning (*polite*)	1
おふろ	bath	1
おへんじ	reply	10
おべんとう	lunch box; packed lunch	1
おぼん	Obon festival	7
おみこし	portable shrine	7
おみやげ	souvenirs	12
おみやまいり	first visit to the shrine	2
おめでとう	congratulations! (*casual*)	1
おめでとうございます	congratulations! (*polite*)	4
おもしろい	interesting; funny	5
おもち	rice cakes	7
おやすみなさい	good night	1
おりがみ	origami	5
オリンピック	Olympics	9
オレンジジュース	orange juice	1
おわり	finish; end (*noun*)	2
おわります	finish; end (*verb*)	10
おんがく	music	8
おんなのこ	girl	12
オンライン	online	10

か	English	Unit
カード	card	12
ガールフレンド	girlfriend	8
かいぎ	meeting	9
かいて（ください）	write (please)	1
かいます	buy	10
かいもの	shopping	9
かえります	return	12
かがくぶ	science club	10
かぎかっこ	Japanese quotation marks (「　」)	5
かきます	write; draw	10

がくえん	school	1
がくしょく	school food	1
かけじく	Japanese scroll; wall hanging	1
かけぶとん	quilt	1
かけます	sprinkle	6
かしこまりました	certainly	2
かして（ください）	lend (please)	1
かぞえます	count	2
かぞく	family	4
カタログ	catalogue	11
かちます	win	12
月	month	7
かつおぶし	bonito flakes (dried fish flakes)	6
がっこう	school	7
かどう	flower arranging	8
カナダ	Canada	3
かに	crab	5
かぶと	samurai helmet	8
かめ	turtle	4
カメラ	camera	10
火曜日	Tuesday	7
から	from	3
カラオケ	karaoke	8
からて（どう）	(the art of) karate	8
カルフォルニア	California	3
カレーうどん	curry noodle soup	1
カレーライス	curry and rice	1
カレンダー	calendar	7
かわいい	cute; pretty	4
かわいそう	what a pity	11
カンガルー	kangaroo	4
かんげいかい	welcome party	1
がんばって!	good luck! try hard!	1

き	English	Unit
きいて　（ください）	listen (please)	1
きいろ	yellow	12
ききます	listen	10
きじ	pheasant	5
きた	came (*casual*)	5
ギター	guitar	8

きつね	fox	5
きつねうどん	hot noodle soup with fried bean curd	1
きて（ください）	come (please)	8
きのう	yesterday	12
きびだんご	dumplings	5
きます	come	3
キャベツ	cabbage	6
キャラメル	caramel	10
キャンセル	cancel	10
キャンプ	camp; school camp	7
キャンプファイアー	camp fire	8
キャンベラ	Canberra	3
九	nine	2
九さい	9 years old	2
休日	holiday	7
きゅうしょく	school lunch	1
きゅうどう	Japanese archery	8
キューバ	Cuba	11
きょう	today	5
きょうかしょ	textbook	10
きょうしつ	classroom	9
きょうそう	competition; race	12
きょねん	last year	12
きらい	dislike; do not like	6
きりつ	stand up	1
きん	gold	5
きんぎょ	goldfish	4
金曜日	Friday	7

く	English	Unit
クール	cool	6
九月	September	7
くさ	grass	5
くさい	smelly	2
ください	please	1
くだもの	fruit	6
くつ	shoes	10
クッキー	cookie; biscuit	12
くつばこ	shoe cupboard	1
くみ；ぐみ	team	12

クラシック	classic	8
クラス	class	12
クラブ	club	10
クラブかつどう	after-school club activities	10
クラブハウス	clubhouse	11
グランドファイナル	grand final	11
グリークラブ	glee club	10
クリケット	cricket	8
クリスマス	Christmas	6
クリスマスの日	Christmas Day	7
くるま	car	9
くん	Mr	1

け	English	Unit
ケアンズ	Cairns	3
けいしょく	light meals	1
けいたい	mobile phone	3
ケイタイサイト	mobile (web)site	10
けいたい　でんわ	mobile phone	2
ケーキ	cake	6
ケープタウン	Cape Town	3
ゲーム	game	4
ゲスト	guest	4
月曜日	Monday	7
けど	but	2
げんかん	entrance	1
げんき	well; lively	10
けんどう	kendo	2
けんぽうきねん日	Constitution Day	7

こ	English	Unit
五	five	2
ご	language	8
コアラ	koala	4
ごあんない	announcement	2
こいのぼり	carp kites	7
ごうけい	total	2

ISBN 9780170196826

こうこう	senior high school	1
こうちゃ	English (black) tea	6
こうはい	junior students	1
コーチ	coach	12
コーヒー	coffee	6
コーラ	cola	1
ゴール	goal	10
ゴールデンウィーク	Golden Week	7
ゴールドコースト	Gold Coast	12
コーンフレーク	cornflakes	6
五月	May	7
ここ	here	2
ココア	cocoa	1
九日	9th day of the month	7
コスプレ	costume play	11
ごちそうさま	thanks (after a meal)	1
こと	thing	8
こどもの日	Children's Day	7
ごはん	rice (boiled); meal	1
こぶた	piglet	5
こむぎこ	plain flour	6
コメディアン	comedian	12
ごめんなさい	sorry; I'm sorry	5
ごめんね	sorry (casual)	9
ごもくごはん	rice cooked with five other ingredients	1
ゴルフ	golf	8
これ	this	3
これから	from now	9
コロッケ	croquette	6
こわい	scary	5
コンサート	concert	9
コンテスト	contest	12
こんにちは	hello; good afternoon	1
コンビニ	convenience store	1
コンピューター	computer	6

さ	English	Unit
サーフィン	surfing	8
サーフコンペ	surf competition	11
さい	years old	2
サイクリング	cycling	12
さいご	last	10
さいごに	lastly	8
サイト	site (website)	11
ざいりょう	ingredients	6
さかな	fish	5
さくぶん	essay; composition	10
さしみ	sashimi	6
サッカー	soccer	2
ざっし	magazines	10
さどう	tea ceremony	8
さむらい	samurai	8
さようなら	goodbye	1
サラダ	salad	6
サラダオイル	salad oil	6
さる	monkey	5
さん	Mr; Mrs; Miss	1
三	three	2
三月	March	7
サンドイッチ	sandwich	1
ざんねん	bad luck; that's a pity	4
さんねんせい	third-year student	1
三りんしゃきょうそう	tricycle race	12

し	English	Unit
四	four	2
しあい	match; game	8
シーディー	CD	10
シェフ	chef	12
四月	April	7
じかん	time	4
しきぶとん	mattress	1
しけん	exam	12
じこしょうかい	self-introduction	3
じしょ	dictionary	10
しずかに	be quiet	1

ISBN 9780170196826

しずかに して（ください）	be quiet (please)	1
七 (しち)	seven	2
七月 (しちがつ)	July	7
七五三 (しちごさん)	Shichigosan festival	2
しって います	know	5
しつもん	question	4
して（ください）	do it (please)	1
じてんしゃ	bicycle	9
シドニー (しどにー)	Sydney	3
シネマ (しねま)	cinema	11
します	do; play	5
しめて （ください）	close it (please)	1
ジャカルタ (じゃかるた)	Jakarta	3
しゃしん	photo; photography	10
じゃね	see you (casual)	11
しゃぶしゃぶ	a meat and vegetable dish	6
じゃまた	see you later (casual)	6
十 (じゅう)	ten	2
十一月 (じゅういちがつ)	November	7
しゅうがく りょこう	school trip	12
十月 (じゅうがつ)	October	7
十三まいり (じゅうさんまいり)	celebration for 13-year-old children	2
じゅうじつ	jujitsu	8
ジュース (じゅーす)	juice	6
じゅうどう	judo	8
十二月 (じゅうにがつ)	December	7
しゅうまつ	weekend	9
十四日 (じゅうよっか)	14th day of the month	7
じゅく	tutoring	1
しゅくだい	homework	10
じゅけん	senior high school entrance exams	1
しゅみ	hobby; interest	8
しょうかい	introduction	4
しょうがつ	New Year	7
しょうがっこう	primary school	1
しょうじょまんが	girls' comic books	11
じょうず	good at	8
しょうねんまんが	boys' comic books	11
じょうば	horse-riding	8

しょうわの日 (しょうわのひ)	Showa Emperor's Birthday	7
しょくどう	canteen	1
しょどう	calligraphy	8
しります	know	4
しろ	white	12
人 (じん)	person; people	3
シンガポール (しんがぽーる)	Singapore	3
しんかんせん	bullet train	9
じんじゃ	Shinto shrine	12
ジンジャーエール (じんじゃえーる)	ginger ale	11
しんじられない	that's unbelievable	8
しんぶん	newspaper	10

す	English	Unit
すいえい	swimming	8
すいえいたいかい	swimming carnival	7
すいえいぶ	swimming club	10
すいそうがくぶ	symphonic winds club	10
水曜日 (すいようび)	Wednesday	7
スウェーデン (すうぇーでん)	Sweden	11
スーパー (すーぱー)	supermarket	12
スーパースター (すーぱーすたー)	superstar	8
スカイプ (すかいぷ)	Skype	10
すき	like	6
スキー (すきー)	ski; skiing	8
すき じゃない	dislike; do not like	9
すきやき	beef hot pot	6
すぐ	soon	5
スクーター (すくーたー)	scooter	9
スクリーンショット (すくりーんしょっと)	screen shot	10
スケート (すけーと)	skate; skating	6
スケートボード (すけーとぼーど)	skateboard	8
スケジュール (すけじゅーる)	schedule	7
スコア (すこあ)	score	4
すごい	incredible; amazing	1
すこし	little; a little	8
すし	sushi	1
すずめ	sparrow	5
スター (すたー)	star	8

ISBN 9780170196826

スタート	start	10
スタバ	Starbucks	10
ステーキ	steak	8
すてき	cool; wonderful	8
ストロベリー	strawberry	6
すのもの	cucumber in a vinegar dressing	1
スパゲッティ	spaghetti	9
スピーチ	speech	10
スポーツ	sports	8
スポーツ センター	sports centre	9
すみません	excuse me; I'm sorry	1
すもう	sumo wrestling	4
すわって（ください）	sit (please)	1
すんで います	live	3

せ	English	Unit
せいじんの日	Coming-of-Age Day	2
せいと	students	10
せいばつ	punish	5
セール	sale	11
せつぶん	Setsubun festival	7
せつめい	explanation	1
ゼロ	zero	4
せんげつ	last month	12
せんしゅう	last week	12
せんせい	teacher	1
ぜんぜん □ません	not at all	6
せんぱい	senior students	1

そ	English	Unit
そうじ	cleaning	1
そう　しましょう	let's do that	11
そう　です	that's right; that's so	4
ソース	sauce	6
ソーセージ	sausage	6
そして	and; also; as well as	5
そつぎょうしき	graduation ceremony	12
そつぎょう しょうしょ	graduation certificate	12
その	that (one there)	9
そのほか	other	9

そば	noodles	1
ソフト	software	10
ソフトボール	softball	8
それ	that (one there)	11
それから	and then; and also	5
それは　ちょっと...	I do not really want to	11

た	English	Unit
ダーウィン	Darwin	3
たいいくの日	Sports Day	7
だいがく	university	1
だいきらい	hate	6
だいじ	important	6
だいじょうぶ	okay; all right	9
だいすき	love; really like	6
たいそう	gymnastics	8
タイプ	type	8
たいへん！	oh no!	8
ダウンロード	download	10
たかい	expensive	11
だから	therefore; that's why	10
たからじま	treasure island	4
たくさん	a lot	11
タクシー	taxi	6
だして	take out	1
たたみ	floor matting	1
たっきゅう	table tennis	10
たって（ください）	stand up (please)	1
たなばた	Tanabata festival	7
たぬき	racoon dog	5
たのしい	fun; enjoyable	11
たのしみ	looking forward to it	9
タブ	tab	10
たべて（ください）	eat (please)	6
たべます	eat	5
たべもの	food	6
たまご	egg	6
たまごやき	omelette	1
だめ	not allowed	3
だれ	who	3
だれの	whose	5
たんじょうび	birthday	7
ダンス	dance; dancing	8
ダンスパーティー	dance party	7

ISBN 9780170196826

ち	English	Unit
ちいさい	small	5
チーズ	cheese	6
チーズバーガーコンボ	cheeseburger combo	9
チーム	team	11
ちがいます	that is not right	4
チキン	chicken	6
ちとせあめ	thousand-year candy	2
ちゃくせき	sit	1
ちゃそば	tea-flavoured noodles	6
チャット	(Internet) chat	8
ちゃん	Mr; Miss	1
チャンピオン	champion	4
ちゅうがく	junior high school	1
ちゅうがっこう	junior high school	1
ちゅうごくご	Chinese	8
ちょうじゅのいわい	celebration of long life	2
チョコチーズケーキ	chocolate cheesecake	6
チョコレート	chocolate	6
ちょっと まって（ください）	wait a moment (please)	1

て	English	Unit
ディーヴィーディー	DVD	10
ていしょく	set meal; set menu	1
ディズニーランド	Disneyland	9
デート	date	12
てがみ	letter	10
できあがり	it's finished	6
テキスト	textbook; text	1
できます	can; can do; can play	8
です	it is; I am; this is; it has	1
テスト	test	7
テニス	tennis	8
デパート	department store	9
でも	but; however	5
デモンストレーション	demonstration	12
てりやきチキン	teriyaki chicken	6
テレビ	television	10
てん	points; comma (、)	4
でんしゃ	train	9
てんぷら	deep-fried seafood and vegetables	1
でんわ	telephone	2
でんわ して（ください）	call (please); telephone (please)	11
でんわ ばんごう	telephone number	2

つ	English	Unit
一日	1st day of the month	7
つかれた!	I'm tired!	12
つぎ	next	3
つきみそば	hot noodle soup with raw egg	1
つくりかた	method; how to make	6
つくります	make	10
つけもの	pickles	1
つなひき	tug of war	12
つまらない	boring	11
つゆ	rainy season	7

と	English	Unit
ドア	door	1
ドイツ	Germany	8
どう	how	4
どうして	why	12
どうじょう	gymnasium	8
どうぞ	here you are	2
どうぞ よろしく	pleased to meet you	1
どうぶつ	animal	5
どうぶつあいご しゅうかん	Animal Welfare Week	5
どうぶつあいごの日	animal welfare day	5
どうも	thanks	1
どうも ありがとう	thank you	1
どうも ありがとう ございました	thank you very much	8
とうろう	lanterns	7
十日	10th day of the month	7

二百四十八

248 Glossary

ISBN 9780170196826

トースト	toast	6
ドーナツ	donuts	6
とおり	path	5
とき	time	11
ときどき	sometimes	8
どくしょ	reading	8
どこ	where	3
ところで	by the way	12
とし	years; age	2
としょかん	library	12
とって（ください）	take [a photo] (please)	12
とても	very	10
ともだち	friend	3
土曜日	Saturday	7
ドラキュラ	Dracula	12
ドラゴン	dragon	5
ドラマ	drama	12
とり	bird	4
とります	take; record	10
ドリンク	drink	1
トロント	Toronto	3
とんかつ	pork, crumbed and deep-fried	12
どんな	what kind	1

な	English	Unit
中	middle	1
なっとう	sticky fermented soya beans	1
なつ休み	summer holidays	12
七	seven	2
なに	what	5
七日	7th day of the month	7
なまえ	name	3
なるほど	indeed	5
なん	what	2
なん月	what month	7
なんさい	how old	2
なんで	by what means; how	9
なん日	what date	7
なん人	how many people	4
なん曜日	what day	7

に	English	Unit
二月	February	7
にく	meat	5
二十四日	24th day of the month	7
二だん	level 2	3
日	day	3
日曜日	Sunday	7
について	about	10
にっき	diary	10
日本	Japan	1
にもの	simmered chicken and pork	1
にゅうがくしき	school entrance ceremony	12
ニュージーランド	New Zealand	3
ニューヨーク	New York	3
にんげんピラミッド	human pyramid	12
にんじん	carrot	6

ぬ	English	Unit
ヌードル	noodle	10

ね	English	Unit
ね	isn't it?	11
ねぎ	shallots; spring onions	6
ねこ	cat	4
ねずみ	mouse	5
ネットボール	netball	8
ねます	sleep	10
ねんがじょう	New Year's cards	7

の	English	Unit
ノート	notebook; note	1
のこして（ください）	leave it (please)	2
のこします	leave (something behind)	2
のせます	put on top	6
のみます	drink (verb)	5
のみもの	drink (noun)	6
のり	dried seaweed	1
のります	catch; ride; get on	12

ISBN 9780170196826

は	English	Unit
バーゲン	bargain	11
パース	Perth	3
パーティー	party	7
パートナー	partner	8
バーベキュー	barbeque	11
はい	yes	1
はいって（ください）	come in (please)	9
バイバイ	bye bye	2
はいります	enter; go into	12
はし	chopsticks	6
はじめ	start; beginning	2
はじめて	for the first time	12
はじめまして	how do you do	1
パジャマ	pyjama	11
ばしょ	venue; place	11
バス	bus	9
バスケットボール	basketball	8
パスタ	pasta	6
二十	20 years old	2
はち	eight	2
八月	August	7
はちみつ	honey	1
二十日	20th day of the month	7
はなし	talk; story	5
はなします	speak; talk	10
バナナ	banana	12
はなび	fireworks	7
はなみ	spring cherry blossom viewing	7
バニラ	vanilla	6
バニラシェイク	vanilla shake	11
ははの日	Mothers' Day	7
パフェ	parfait	6
ハム	ham	6
はやく	quickly	1
バリ	Bali	3
パリ	Paris	3
ハリウッド	Hollywood	3
はる休み	spring holiday	12

	English	Unit
バレーボール	volleyball	8
ばん	evening; night	11
パン	bread	5
パンくいきょうそう	bread-eating competition	12
バンクーバー	Vancouver	3
ばんぐみ	programme	10
ばんごう	number	2
ばんごはん	dinner	6
バンジージャンプ	bungee jump	12
パンダ	panda	5
バンド	band	10
ハンバーガー	hamburger	6

ひ	English	Unit
日	day	1
ピアノ	piano	8
ひがわり　ていしょく	set menu of the day	1
ピクニック	picnic	9
ひこうき	aeroplane	9
ピザ	pizza	6
ひさしぶり　ですね	long time no see	10
びじゅつ	art	10
びじゅつぶ	visual arts club	10
ビスケット	biscuit	5
ひっくり　かえします	flip over	6
びっくり　しました	was surprised	12
ぴったり	correct; just so	8
ヒップホップ	hip-hop	8
ビデオ	video	4
ビデオクリップ	video clip	10
ひどい	disgusting	5
一つ	one (thing)	5
一人	one person	4
一人っこ	only child	4
一人で	by oneself; alone	9
ひなにんぎょう	Hina dolls	7
ひなまつり	Doll's Festival	7
ひまな　とき	free time	11
ひみつ	secret	9

ISBN 9780170196826

びょういん	hospital	5
びょうき	aeroplane	5
ピラミッド	pyramid	10
ひる	noon	11
ひるごはん	lunch	6
ひる休み	lunchtime	6
ピンク	pink	12
ビンテージ	vintage	12
ビンテージセール	vintage sale	12

ふ	English	Unit
ぶ	club	10
ファイル	file	10
ファッション	fashion	10
ファミコン	family computer	11
ファミリー	family	9
ファンタ	Fanta	1
ファンタジー	fantasy	9
フィギュアスケート	figure skate	11
フィンランド	Finland	11
プール	pool	11
フェイスブック	Facebook	10
フェスティバル	festival	11
フェリー	ferry	9
フェンシング	fencing	11
フォルダー	folder	10
ぶかつ	after-school club activities	10
ふく	clothes	10
ふじさん	Mount Fuji	3
二人	two people	4
二日	2nd day of the month	7
ブックマーク	bookmark	10
フットボール	football	9
ふとん	futon	1
ふね	ship	9
ふゆ休み	winter holiday	12
フライパン	frying pan	6

ブラジリア	Brasilia	3
フラペチーノ	frappuccino	10
フランス	France	3
ふりかけて（ください）	sprinkle on (please)	6
ブリスベン	Brisbane	3
ふりそで	long-sleeved kimono	2
プレゼント	present	2
ふろしき	Japanese wrapping cloth	1
ふろば	bathroom	1
プロファイル	profile	10
ぶんか	culture	10
ぶんかさい	cultural festival	4
ぶんかの日	Culture Day	7

へ	English	Unit
へ	to; dear (in letters)	9
へた	unskilful	8
ペット	pet	4
へび	snake	4
ヘルプ	help	10
ペン	pen	1
べんきょう	study	1
へんじ	reply	10
ペンパル	penpal	11
べんろんぶ	debating club	10

ほ	English	Unit
ほうそうぶ	broadcasting club	10
ボーイフレンド	boyfriend	9
ボート	boat	9
ホーム	home	10
ホームページ	homepage	10
ホームルーム	homeroom	10
ほかに	something else; another	9
ぼく	I; me (boys)	1
ホストシスター	host sister	12

ほすとふぁーざー ホストファーザー	host father	12
ほすとふぁみりー ホストファミリー	host family	11
ほすとまざー ホストマザー	host mother	12
ほっけー ホッケー	hockey	8
ほっとどっぐ ホットドッグ	hot dog	5
ぽっぷこーん ポップコーン	popcorn	10
ぽっぷみゅーじっく ポップ ミュージック	pop music	8
ぽてとちっぷす ポテトチップス	potato chips	8
ほてる ホテル	hotel	12
ほばーと ホバート	Hobart	3
ほん 本	book	1
ぼんおどり	Obon folk dancing	7
ほんとう?	really? truly?	8

ま	English	Unit
まいこさん	geisha	12
まいにち	every day	6
まえ; まえに	before; in front of	11
まくら	pillow	1
まずい	tastes awful	11
まぜます	mix; stir	6
また	again	4
また あした	see you tomorrow	1
またね	see you later	1
まち	town	9
まちます	wait	1
まっちゃ	green tea	6
まって います	I am waiting	10
まって (ください)	wait (please)	1
まつり	festival	7
まで	until	10
まど	window	1
まねーじゃー マネージャー	manager	12
まねきねこ	welcome cat	12
まよねーず マヨネーズ	mayonnaise	6
まらそん マラソン	marathon	10
まる	full stop (。)	5
まるを して (ください)	circle it (please)	7
まんが	cartoon; comic book	1
まんざい	comic dialogue	12

み	English	Unit
みず 水	water	5
みすゆにばーす ミスユニバース	Miss Universe	10
みせ	shop	12
みせて (ください)	show it (please)	1
みそしる	miso soup	1
みっか 三日	3rd day of the month	7
みて (ください)	look (please)	1
みどりの日 ひ	Greenery Day	7
みなさん	everyone	1
みます	watch; look at	10
みゅーじっく ミュージック	music	8
みるく ミルク	milk	6
みんと ミント	mint	6
みんな	everyone; all	12
みんなで	with everyone	4

む	English	Unit
むいか 六日	6th day of the month	7
むかしむかし	once upon a time	5
むかできょうそう	centipede race	12
むずかしい	difficult	11

め	English	Unit
めいし	business card	2
めーとる メートル	metre	12
めーる メール	email	10
めっせーじ メッセージ	message	2
めでたし、めでたし	they all lived happily ever after	5
めにゅー メニュー	menu	1
めも メモ	memo	3
めもりー メモリー	memory	10
めるぼるん メルボルン	Melbourne	3

ISBN 9780170196826

も	English	Unit
もう	another; more	4
もう　いちど	once more	1
モーニングティー	morning tea	10
木曜日	Thursday	7
もしもし	hello (on the phone)	2
もち	rice cakes	7
もの	thing	6
もも	peach	5

や	English	Unit
やきおにぎり	fried rice balls	6
やきそば	fried noodles	6
やきとり	grilled chicken	6
やきます	grill; fry	6
やきゅう	baseball	8
やさい	vegetables	5
やさしい	easy	11
やすい	cheap	11
休み	holiday; rest	7
やっぱり	just as I thought	8
山	mountain	1

ゆ	English	Unit
ユーチューブ	YouTube	10

よ	English	Unit
よいしょ!	push! heave!	8
八日	8th day of the month	7
ようこそ	welcome	1
ヨーグルト	yoghurt	10
よかった	was good	8
よく	often	8
四日	4th day of the month	7
ヨット	yacht	9
よみます	read	10
より	from	9
よる	night; evening	11
よろしく	pleased to meet you	1
四	four	2
よんで（ください）	read (please)	1

ら	English	Unit
ラーメン	Chinese-style noodle soup	1
ラグビー	rugby	8
ラジオ	radio	10
ラップ	rap	10
ラムレーズン	rum and raisin	6

り	English	Unit
りくじょう	athletics	10
りくじょうぶ	athletics club	12
りょうり	cooking	8
りょかん	Japanese-style inn	12
りょこう	trip; holiday; travel	12
リレー	relay	12

る	English	Unit
ルームナンバー	room number	2

れ	English	Unit
れい	zero; bow	2
レストラン	restaurant	9
レモネード	lemonade	1
レモン	lemon	1
れんしゅう	practice	10

ろ	English	Unit
ローラーコースター	rollercoaster	12
ローラーブレード	rollerblade	8
ロールプレー	role-play	1
六	six	2
ログアウト	log out	10
ログイン	log in	10
六月	June	7
ロック	rock (music)	8
ロック　コンサート	rock concert	9

二百五十三

ISBN 9780170196826

わ	English	Unit
ワールドカップ	world cup	11
ワイヤレス	wireless	10
わがし	Japanese sweets	6
わかります	understand	2
わさび	wasabi	6
わしょく	Japanese food	6
わたし	I; me	1
わたしたち	we; us	12
わたしの	my	4
ワンピース	one piece; dress	10

えいご～日本ご
English–Japanese

A	Japanese	Unit
about	について	10
according to taste	おこのみに	6
account	アカウント	10
Adelaide	アデレード	3
aeroplane	ひこうき	5
after	あとで; あと	9
after-school club activities	クラブかつどう; ぶかつ	10
after that	それから	5
afterwards	あとで	9
again	また	4
age	とし	3
aikido	あいきどう	8
all	みんな	12
alone	一人で	9
also	そして	5
always	いつも	8
amazing	すごい	1
America	アメリカ	3
American person	アメリカ人	3
and	そして	5
and then; and also	それから	5
animal	どうぶつ	5
animal food	えさ	5
animal welfare day	どうぶつあいごの日	5

	Japanese	Unit
Animal Welfare Week	どうぶつあいごしゅうかん	5
animated movie	アニメ	10
announcement	ごあんない	2
apple juice	アップルジュース	1
application	アプリケーション; アプリ	10
April	四月	7
archery	アーチェリー	11
art	びじゅつ	10
as well as	そして	5
as you like; according to taste	おこのみに	6
athletics	りくじょう	10
athletics carnival	うんどうかい	7
athletics club	りくじょうぶ	12
Auckland	オークランド	3
August	八月	7
aunt	おばさん	9
Australia	オーストラリア	3
Australian rules football	オーストラリアンフットボール	8
Autumn Festival	あきまつり	7

ISBN 9780170196826

B	Japanese	Unit
baby	あかちゃん	4
bad luck	ざんねん	4
Bali	バリ	3
banana	バナナ	12
band	バンド	10
barbeque	バーベキュー	11
bargain	バーゲン	11
baseball	やきゅう	8
basketball	バスケットボール	8
bath	おふろ	1
bathroom	ふろば	1
be	います	4
beach	うみ	9
beef hot pot	すきやき	6
before	まえに；まえ	11
beginning	はじめ	2
be quiet (please)	しずかに；しずかにして（ください）	1
bicycle	じてんしゃ	9
big	おおきい	5
bird	とり	4
birthday	たんじょうび；おたんじょうび	2
biscuit	クッキー；ビスケット	12
blue	あお	12
boat	ボート	9
bonito flakes (dried fish flakes)	かつおぶし	6
book	本	1
bookmark	ブックマーク	10
boring	つまらない	11
boyfriend	ボーイフレンド	9
Brasilia	ブラジリア	3
bread	パン	6
bread-eating competition	パンくいきょうそう	12
breakfast	あさごはん	6
Brisbane	ブリスベン	3
broadcasting club	ほうそうぶ	10
bullet train	しんかんせん	9
bungee jump	バンジージャンプ	12

	Japanese	Unit
bus	バス	9
business card	めいし	2
busy	いそがしい	10
but	でも；けど	2
buy	かいます	10
bye bye	バイバイ	2
by oneself	一人で	9
by the way	ところで	12
by what means (how)	なんで	9

C	Japanese	Unit
cabbage	キャベツ	6
Cairns	ケアンズ	3
cake	ケーキ	6
calendar	カレンダー	7
California	カルフォルニア	3
call (please); telephone (please)	でんわ　して（ください）	11
calligraphy	しょどう	8
camera	カメラ	10
camp	キャンプ	7
camp fire	キャンプ　ファイアー	8
can; can do	できます	8
Canada	カナダ	3
Canberra	キャンベラ	3
cancel	キャンセル	10
canteen	しょくどう	1
Cape Town	ケープタウン	3
car	くるま	9
caramel	キャラメル	10
card	カード	12
carp kites	こいのぼり	7
carrot	にんじん	6
cartoon	まんが	1
cat	ねこ	4
catalogue	カタログ	11
catch (e.g. a bus)	のります	12
CD	シーディー	10
celebration for 13-year-old children	十三まいり	2

English	Japanese	Ch.
celebration of long life	ちょうじゅのいわい	2
certainly	かしこまりました	2
centipede race	むかできょうそう	12
champion	チャンピオン	4
chat (Internet)	チャット	8
cheap	やすい	11
cheer	おうえん	12
cheese	チーズ	6
cheeseburger combo	チーズバーガーコンボ	9
chef	シェフ	12
chicken	チキン	6
Children's Day	こどもの日	7
Chinese	ちゅうごくご	8
chocolate	チョコレート	6
chocolate cheesecake	チョコチーズケーキ	6
chopsticks	おはし; はし	1
Christmas	クリスマス	6
Christmas Day	クリスマスの日	7
cinema	シネマ; えいがかん	11
circle it (please)	まるを して (ください)	7
class	クラス	12
classic	クラシック	8
classroom	きょうしつ	9
cleaning	そうじ	1
close it (please)	しめて (ください)	1
clothes	ふく	10
club	クラブ; ぶ	10
clubhouse	クラブハウス	11
coach	コーチ	12
cocoa	ココア	1
coffee	コーヒー	6
cola	コーラ	1
come	きます	3
come (please)	きて (ください)	8

English	Japanese	Ch.
comedian	コメディアン	12
come in	いらっしゃい	10
come in (please)	はいって (ください)	9
come in quickly!	はやく はいって!	9
comic books	まんが; しょうねんまんが (boys); しょうじょまんが (girls)	1
comic dialogue	まんざい	12
Coming-of-Age Day	せいじんの日	2
comma	てん (、)	5
competition	きょうそう	12
composition; essay	さくぶん	10
computer	コンピューター	6
concert	コンサート	9
congratulations!	おめでとう (casual); おめでとう ございます (polite)	1
Constitution Day	けんぽうきねん日	7
contest	コンテスト	12
convenience store	コンビニ	1
cookie	クッキー	12
cooking	りょうり	8
cool	クール; すてき	6
cornflakes	コーンフレーク	6
correct; just so	ぴったり	8
costume play	コスプレ	11
count	かぞえます	2
crab	かに	5
cricket	クリケット	8
croquette	コロッケ	6
Cuba	キューバ	11
cucumber in a vinegar dressing	すのもの	1
cultural festival	ぶんかさい	4
culture	ぶんか	10
Culture Day	ぶんかの日	7
cupboard for futon	おしいれ	1
curry and rice	カレーライス	1
cute	かわいい	4
cycling	サイクリング	12

ISBN 9780170196826

D	Japanese	Unit
dance; dancing	ダンス	8
dance party	ダンスパーティー	7
Darwin	ダーウィン	3
dash	ぼう　（ー）	6
date	デート	12
day	日	1
dear (*in letters*); to	へ	9
debating club	べんろんぶ	10
December	十二月	7
deep-fried seafood and vegetables	てんぷら	1
delicious	おいしい	6
demonstration	デモンストレーション	12
department store	デパート	9
devil	おに	5
diary	にっき	10
dictionary	じしょ	10
difficult	むずかしい	11
dinner	ばんごはん	6
disgusting	ひどい	5
dislike; do not like	きらい；　すき じゃない	6
Disneyland	ディズニーランド	9
do	します	5
do it (please)	して（ください）	1
dog	いぬ	4
Doll's Festival	ひなまつり	7
donuts	ドーナツ	6
door	ドア	1
download	ダウンロード	10
Dracula	ドラキュラ	12
dragon	ドラゴン	5
drama	ドラマ；　えんげき	10
drama club	えんげきぶ	10
dress	ワンピース	10
dried seaweed	のり	1
drink (*verb*)	のみます	5
drink (*noun*)	のみもの；ドリンク	1
duck	あひる	4
dumplings	きびだんご	5
DVD	ディーヴィーディー	10

E	Japanese	Unit
Easter	イースター	7
easy	やさしい	11
eat	たべます	5
eat (please)	たべて（ください）	6
ebook	イーブック	10
eel	うなぎ	6
egg	たまご	6
eight	はち	2
email	メール	10
emu	エミュー	11
end	おわり (*noun*);　おわります (*verb*)	2
end; the end	おしまい	5
English language	えいご	8
English (black) tea	こうちゃ	6
enjoyable	たのしい	11
enter	はいります	12
entrance	げんかん	1
essay	さくぶん	10
evening	ばん；　よる	11
event	イベント	11
every day	まいにち	6
everyone	みなさん；　みんな	1
exam	しけん	12
excursion	えんそく	6
excuse me	すみません	1
expensive	たかい	11
explanation	せつめい	1
extra	エクストラ	10

F	Japanese	Unit
Facebook	フェイスブック	10
family computer	かぞく；　ファミリー	4
family	ファミコン	11
Fanta	ファンタ	1
fantasy	ファンタジー	9
fashion	ファッション	10
father	おとうさん	4
February	二月	7
fencing	フェンシング	11
ferry	フェリー	9

二百五十七

ISBN 9780170196826

English	Japanese	Unit
festival	まつり；フェスティバル	7
figure skate	フィギュアスケート	11
file	ファイル	10
finish	おわり (noun)；おわります (verb)	2
finished; it's finished	できあがり	6
Finland	フィンランド	11
fireworks	はなび	7
first time (for the)	はじめて	12
first visit to the shrine	おみやまいり	2
first-year students	一ねんせい	12
fish	さかな	5
five	五	2
flavour	あじ	1
flip over	ひっくり かえします	6
floor matting	たたみ	1
flower arranging	かどう；いけばな	8
folder	フォルダー	10
food	たべもの	6
foot (on); walking	あるいて	9
football	フットボール	9
four	四；四	2
fox	きつね	5
France	フランス	3
frappuccino	フラペチーノ	10
free time	ひまな とき	11
Friday	金曜日	7
fried noodles	やきそば	6
fried rice balls	やきおにぎり	6
friend	ともだち	3
from	から；より	3
from now	これから	9
fruit	くだもの	6
fry; grill	やきます	6
frying pan	フライパン	6
full stop	まる （。）	5
fun	たのしい	11
funny; interesting	おもしろい	5
funny; strange	おかしい	5
futon	ふとん	1

G	Japanese	Unit
game	ゲーム；しあい	4
geek	おたく	11
geisha	まいこさん	12
Germany	ドイツ	8
get on (e.g. a bus)	のります	12
ginger ale	ジンジャーエール	11
girl	おんなのこ	12
girlfriend	ガールフレンド	8
glee club	グリークラブ	10
go	いきます	5
goal	ゴール	10
gold	きん	5
Gold Coast	ゴールドコースト	12
Golden Week	ゴールデンウィーク	7
goldfish	きんぎょ	4
golf	ゴルフ	8
good	いい	5
good afternoon	こんにちは	1
good at	じょうず	8
goodbye	さようなら	1
good luck! try hard!	がんばって! (casual)	1
good morning	おはよう (casual)；おはようございます (polite)	1
good night	おやすみなさい	1
graduation ceremony	そつぎょうしき	12
graduation certificate	そつぎょうしょうしょ	12
grandfather	おじいさん	4
grand final	グランドファイナル	11
grandmother	おばあさん	4
grass	くさ	5
Greenery Day	みどりの日	7
green tea	おちゃ；まっちゃ	1
grill; fry	やきます	6
grilled chicken	やきとり	6
guest	ゲスト	4
guitar	ギター	8
gymnasium	どうじょう	8
gymnastics	たいそう	8

ISBN 9780170196826

H	Japanese	Unit
ham	ハム	6
hamburger	ハンバーガー	6
happy	うれしい	2
happy birthday	おたんじょうび おめでとう	2
hate	だいきらい	6
haunted house	おばけやしき	12
have	います	4
heave!	よいしょ!	8
hello	こんにちは もしもし (on the phone)	1
help	ヘルプ	10
here you are	どうぞ	2
Hina dolls	ひなにんぎょう	7
hip-hop	ヒップホップ	8
Hobart	ホバート	3
hobby	しゅみ	8
hockey	ホッケー	8
holiday	休日; 休み	7
Hollywood	ハリウッド	3
home	うち; ホーム	9
homepage	ホームページ	10
homeroom	ホームルーム	10
homework	しゅくだい	10
honey	はちみつ	1
horse	うま	4
horse-riding	じょうば	8
hospital	びょういん	5
host family	ホストファミリー	11
host father	ホストファーザー	12
host mother	ホストマザー	12
host sister	ホストシスター	12
hot dog	ホットドッグ	5
hotel	ホテル	12
house	うち	9
how; by what means	なんで	9
how are you?	おげんき ですか	10
how do you do	はじめまして	1
however	でも	5
human pyramid	にんげんピラミッド	12

I	Japanese	Unit
I; me	わたし; ぼく(boys)	1
ice-cream	アイスクリーム	6
idea	アイディア	11
important	だいじ	6
incredible	すごい	1
indeed	なるほど	5
Indonesia	インドネシア	3
indoor shoes	うわばき	1
ingredients	ざいりょう	6
interest; hobby	しゅみ	8
interesting	おもしろい	5
Internet	インターネット	10
interview	インタビュー	11
introduction	しょうかい	4
iPod	アイポッド	10
is	います	4
isn't it?	ね	11
Italy	イタリア	9

J	Japanese	Unit
Jakarta	ジャカルタ	3
January	一月	7
Japan	日本	1
Japanese archery	きゅうどう	8
Japanese food	わしょく	6
Japanese ladder puzzle	あみだくじ	5
Japanese quotation marks	かぎかっこ（「　」）	5
Japanese scroll	かけじく	1
Japanese sweet (a type of)	あんみつ	6
Japanese sweets	わがし	6
Japanese-style inn	りょかん	12
Japanese wrapping cloth	ふろしき	1
judo	じゅうどう	8
juice	ジュース	6
jujitsu	じゅうじつ	8
July	七月	7
June	六月	7

二百五十九

ISBN 9780170196826

junior high school	ちゅうがっこう；ちゅうがく	1
junior students	こうはい	1
just as I thought	やっぱり	8

K	Japanese	Unit
kangaroo	カンガルー	4
karaoke	カラオケ	8
karate	からて；からてどう	8
kendo (Japanese fencing)	けんどう	2
kimono, long-sleeved	ふりそで	2
know	しって います	5
koala	コアラ	4

L	Japanese	Unit
language	ご	8
lanterns	とうろう	7
large	おおきい	5
last	さいご	10
lastly	さいごに	8
last month	せんげつ	12
last week	せんしゅう	12
last year	きょねん	12
late	おそい	9
later	あとで	9
leave (something behind)	のこします	2
leave it (please)	のこして（ください）	2
lemon	レモン	1
lemonade	レモネード	1
lend (please)	かして（ください）	1
letter	てがみ	10
level 1	一だん	3
level 2	二だん	3
library	としょかん	12
lie	うそ	5
light meals	けいしょく	1
like	すき	6
listen	ききます	1
listen (please)	きいて（ください）	1
little; a little	すこし	8

little; little bit	ちょっと	8
live	すんで います	3
lively	げんき	10
log in	ログイン	10
log out	ログアウト	10
long-sleeved kimono	ふりそで	2
long time no see	ひさしぶり ですね	10
look (please)	みて（ください）	1
look at	みます	10
looking forward to it	たのしみ	9
lots; a lot	たくさん	11
love; really like	だいすき	6
lunch	ひるごはん	6
lunch box	おべんとう	1
lunchtime	ひる休み	6

M	Japanese	Unit
magazines	ざっし	10
make	つくります	10
manager	マネージャー	12
marathon	マラソン	10
March	三月	7
match	しあい	8
mattress	しきぶとん	1
May	五月	7
mayonnaise	マヨネーズ	6
me; I	わたし；ぼく (boys)	1
meal	ごはん	1
meat	にく	5
meet	あいます	10
meeting	かいぎ	9
Melbourne	メルボルン	3
memo	メモ	3
memory	メモリー	10
menu	メニュー	1
message	メッセージ	2
method; how to make	つくりかた	6
metre	メートル	12
middle	中	1
milk	ミルク	6

ISBN 9780170196826

English	Japanese	Unit
mint	ミント	6
miso soup	みそしる	1
Miss Universe	ミスユニバース	10
mix	まぜます	6
mobile phone	けいたい；けいたい　でんわ	2
mobile (web)site	ケイタイサイト	10
Monday	月曜日	7
monkey	さる	5
month	月	7
morning	あさ	11
morning tea	モーニングティー	10
mother	おかあさん	4
Mothers' Day	ははの日	7
mountain	山	1
Mount Fuji	ふじさん	3
mouse	ねずみ	5
movie	えいが	9
music	おんがく；ミュージック	8
my	わたしの	4

N	Japanese	Unit
name	なまえ；おなまえ	3
netball	ネットボール	8
newspaper	しんぶん	10
New Year	おしょうがつ；しょうがつ	7
New Year's cards	ねんがじょう	7
New Year's food	おせちりょうり	6
New York	ニューヨーク	3
New Zealand	ニュージーランド	3
next	つぎ	3
night	ばん；よる	11
nine	九；九	2
no	いいえ	1
noisy	うるさい	5
noodles	うどん；そば；ヌードル	1
noodle soup, Chinese-style	ラーメン	1
noodle soup, curry	カレーうどん	1

English	Japanese	Unit
noodle soup, hot with fried bean curd	きつねうどん	1
noodle soup, hot with raw egg	つきみそば	1
noon	ひる	11
not allowed	だめ	3
not at all	ぜんぜん　□ません	6
note	ノート	1
notebook	ノート	1
not much; not really; not well	あまり；あんまり	6
November	十一月	7
now	いま	8
number	ばんごう	2

O	Japanese	Unit
Obon festival	おぼん	7
Obon folk dancing	ほんおどり	7
ocean	うみ	9
October	十月	7
often	よく	8
ogre	おに	5
ogres	おにども	5
oh no!	たいへん！	8
okay; all right	だいじょうぶ	9
older brother	おにいさん	4
older sister	おねえさん	4
old man; grandfather	おじいさん	4
old woman; grandmother	おばあさん	4
Olympics	オリンピック	9
omelette	たまごやき	1
once	いちど	4
once more	もう　いちど	1
once upon a time	むかしむかし	5
one	一	2
one (thing)	一つ	5
one day	一日	1
one person	一人	4
one semester	一がっき	12
one year	一ねん	7
on foot	あるいて	9
online	オンライン	10

English	Japanese	Unit
only child	一人っこ	4
open it (please)	あけて（ください）	1
orange juice	オレンジジュース	1
origami	おりがみ	5
other	そのほか	9

P	Japanese	Unit
packed lunch	おべんとう	1
pancake, Japanese-style savoury	おこのみやき	6
panda	パンダ	5
parfait	パフェ	6
Paris	パリ	3
partner	パートナー	8
party	パーティー	7
pasta	パスタ	6
path	とおり	5
peach	もも	5
pen	ペン	1
penpal	ペンパル	11
Perth	パース	3
pet	ペット	4
pet food	えさ	5
pheasant	きじ	5
photo; photography	しゃしん	10
piano	ピアノ	8
pickled plums	うめぼし	6
pickles	つけもの	1
picnic	ピクニック	9
piglet	こぶた	5
pillow	まくら	1
pink	ピンク	12
pizza	ピザ	6
place	ばしょ	11
plain flour	こむぎこ	6
play	します	5
please	ください	1
pleased to meet you	どうぞ　よろしく；よろしく	1
points	てん	4
pool	プール	11

P	Japanese	Unit
popcorn	ポップコーン	10
pop music	ポップ　ミュージック	8
pork, crumbed and deep-fried	とんかつ	12
portable shrine	おみこし	7
potato chips	ポテトチップス	8
practice	れんしゅう	10
prawns	えび	6
present	プレゼント	2
pretty	かわいい	4
primary school	しょうがっこう	1
profile	プロファイル	10
programme	ばんぐみ	10
punish	せいばつ	5
push!	よいしょ！	8
put in	いれます	6
put on top	のせます	6
pyjama	パジャマ	11
pyramid	ピラミッド	10

Q	Japanese	Unit
question	しつもん	4
quickly	はやく	1
quiet	しずか	1
quilt	かけぶとん	1

R	Japanese	Unit
rabbit	うさぎ	4
race	きょうそう	12
racoon dog	たぬき	5
radio	ラジオ	10
rainy season	つゆ	7
rap	ラップ	10
read	よみます	10
read (please)	よんで（ください）	1
reading	どくしょ	8
really?	ほんとう？そう　ですか	8
record; take	とります	10
red	あか	12
relay	リレー	12
reply	へんじ；　おへんじ	10
request	おねがい	2

ISBN 9780170196826

rest; holiday	休み	7
restaurant	レストラン	9
return	かえります	12
rice (boiled)	ごはん	1
rice balls	おにぎり	1
rice cakes	もち；　おもち	7
rice cooked with five other ingredients	ごもくごはん	1
rice crackers	あられ	7
ride (e.g. a bus)	のります	12
rock (music)	ロック	8
rock concert	ロック　コンサート	9
role-play	ロールプレー	1
rollerblade	ローラーブレード	8
rollercoaster	ローラーコースター	12
room number	ルームナンバー	2
rugby	ラグビー	8
rum and raisin	ラムレーズン	6

S	Japanese	Unit
salad	サラダ	6
salad oil	サラダオイル	6
sale	セール	11
samurai	さむらい	8
samurai helmet	かぶと	8
sandwich	サンドイッチ	1
sashimi	さしみ	6
Saturday	土曜日	7
sauce	ソース	6
sausage	ソーセージ	6
say (please)	いって（ください）	1
scary	こわい	5
schedule	スケジュール	7
school	がっこう；　がくえん	1
school camp	キャンプ	7
school entrance ceremony	にゅうがくしき	12
school food	がくしょく	1
school lunch	きゅうしょく	1
school trip	しゅうがく　りょこう	12

science club	かがくぶ	10
scooter	スクーター	9
score	スコア	4
screen shot	スクリーンショット	10
seaweed flakes	あおのり	6
secret	ひみつ	9
see	みます	12
see you (casual)	じゃね	11
see you later	またね；　じゃまた	1
see you tomorrow	また　あした	1
self-introduction	じこしょうかい	3
senior high school	こうこう	1
senior high school entrance exams	じゅけん	1
senior students	せんぱい	1
September	九月	7
set meal; set menu	ていしょく	1
set menu of the day	ひがわり　ていしょく	1
Setsubun festival	せつぶん	7
seven	七；　七	2
shallots; spring onions	ねぎ	6
Shichigosan festival	七五三	2
ship	ふね	9
shoe cupboard	くつばこ	1
shoes	くつ	10
shop	みせ	12
shopping	かいもの	9
show it (please)	みせて（ください）	1
Showa Emperor's Birthday	しょうわの日	7
shrine (Shinto)	じんじゃ	12
shut it (please)	しめて（ください）	1
side dishes	おかず	1
Singapore	シンガポール	3
sit	ちゃくせき	1
sit (please)	すわって（ください）	1
site (website)	サイト	11
six	六	2
skate	スケート	6
skateboard	スケートボード	8
skating	スケート	6
ski; skiing	スキー	8

ISBN 9780170196826

Skype	スカイプ	10
sleep	ねます	10
slippers	うわばき	1
small	ちいさい	5
smelly	くさい	2
snake	へび	4
soccer	サッカー	2
softball	ソフトボール	8
software	ソフト	10
sometimes	ときどき	8
soon	すぐ	5
sorry; I'm sorry	ごめんなさい; すみません; ごめんね	5
sorry, I am late	おそく なって すみません	9
souvenirs	おみやげ	12
soya beans, fermented	なっとう	1
soya sauce	おしょうゆ	1
spaghetti	スパゲッティ	9
sparrow	すずめ	5
speak	はなします	10
speech	スピーチ	10
sports	スポーツ	8
sports carnival	うんどうかい	7
sports centre	スポーツ センター	9
Sports Day	たいいくの日	7
spring cherry blossom viewing	はなみ	7
spring holiday	はる休み	12
spring onions	ねぎ	6
sprinkle	かけます	6
sprinkle on (please)	おおじて ふりかけて (ください)	6
stand up	きりつ	1
stand up (please)	たって (ください)	1
star	スター	8
Starbucks	スタバ	10
start; begin	はじめ; スタート	2
steak	ステーキ	8
stir	まぜます	6
story	はなし	5
strange	おかしい	5

strawberry	ストロベリー	6
students	せいと	10
study	べんきょう	1
summer holidays	なつ休み	12
sumo wrestling	すもう	4
Sunday	日曜日	7
supermarket	スーパー	12
superstar	スーパースター	8
surf competition	サーフコンペ	11
surfing	サーフィン	8
survey	アンケート	4
sushi	すし	1
Sweden	スウェーデン	11
sweets	おかし	1
swimming	すいえい	8
swimming carnival	すいえいたいかい	7
swimming club	すいえいぶ	10
Sydney	シドニー	3
symphonic winds club	すいそうがく	10

T	Japanese	Unit
tab	タブ	10
table tennis	たっきゅう	10
take; record	とります	10
take (e.g. a bus)	のります	12
take [a photo] (please)	とって (ください)	12
take out	だして	1
talk (verb)	はなします	10
talk; story (noun)	はなし	5
Tanabata festival	たなばた	7
tastes awful	まずい	11
taxi	タクシー	6
tea ceremony	さどう	8
teacher	せんせい	1
tea-flavoured noodles	ちゃそば	6
team	チーム; くみ; ぐみ	11
telephone	でんわ	2
telephone number	でんわ ばんごう	2
television	テレビ	10

ISBN 9780170196826

temple (Buddhist)	おてら	12
ten	十	2
tennis	テニス	8
teriyaki chicken	てりやきチキン	6
test	テスト	7
textbook	きょうかしょ；テキスト	1
thanks	どうも	1
thanks (after a meal)	ごちそうさま	1
thanks (before a meal)	いただきます	1
thank you	ありがとう；ありがとうございます；どうも　ありがとう	1
thank you for your hard work	おつかれさま	8
thank you very much	どうも　ありがとうございました	2
that (one over there)	あれ	2
that (one there)	その；それ	9
that's a pity	ざんねん	4
that's right	そう　です	4
that's unbelievable	しんじられない	8
therefore	だから	10
they all lived happily ever after	めでたし、めでたし	5
thing	こと；もの	6
third-year student	さんねんせい	1
this	これ	3
thousand-year candy	ちとせあめ	2
three	三	2
Thursday	木曜日	7
time	じかん；とき	4
tired; I'm tired!	つかれた！	12
to; dear (in letters)	へ	9
toast	トースト	6
today	きょう	5
together	いっしょに	11
tomorrow	あした	7
Toronto	トロント	3
total	ごうけい	2
town	まち	9
train	でんしゃ	9
travel	りょこう	12
treasure island	たからじま	4

tricycle race	三りんしゃきょうそう	12
trip	りょこう	12
truly?	ほんとう？	8
Tuesday	火曜日	7
tug of war	つなひき	12
turtle	かめ	4
tutoring	じゅく	1
two people	二人	4
type	タイプ	8

U	Japanese	Unit
unbelievable (that's)	しんじられない	8
understand	わかります	2
United States of America	アメリカ	3
university	だいがく	1
unskilful	へた	8
until	まで	10
upload	アップロード	11

V	Japanese	Unit
Vancouver	バンクーバー	3
vanilla	バニラ	6
vanilla shake	バニラシェイク	11
vegetables	やさい	5
venue	ばしょ	11
very	とても	10
video	ビデオ	4
video clip	ビデオクリップ	10
vintage	ビンテージ	12
vintage sale	ビンテージセール	12
visual arts club	びじゅつぶ	10
volleyball	バレーボール	8

二百六十五

ISBN 9780170196826

W	Japanese	Unit
wait	まちます	1
wait (please)	まって　ください)	1
wait a moment (please)	ちょっと　まって（ください　）	1
waiting (I am)	まって　います	10
wasabi	わさび	6
watch; look at	みます	10
watch (please)	みて（ください）	1
water	水（みず）	5
we; us	わたしたち	12
web	ウェブ（うぇぶ）	10
web design	ウェブデザイン（うぇぶてざいん）	10
website	ウェブサイト（うぇぶさいと）	10
Wednesday	水曜日（すいようび）	7
weekend	しゅうまつ；ウィークエンド（うぃーくえんど）	9
welcome	ようこそ；いらっしゃい	1
welcome cat	まねきねこ	12
welcome party	かんげいかい	1
well; lively	げんき	10
what	なん；　なに	2
what a pity	かわいそう	11
what kind	どんな	1
when	いつ	7
where	どこ	3
white	しろ	12
who	だれ	3
whose	だれの	5
why	どうして	12
Wikipedia	ウィキペディア（うぃきぺてぃあ）	10
win	かちます	12
window	まど	1
winter holiday	ふゆ休み（やす）	12
wireless	ワイヤレス（わいやれす）	10
with everyone	みんなで	4
wonderful	すてき	8
world cup	ワールドカップ（わーるどかっぷ）	11
write; draw	かきます	10
write (please)	かいて（ください）	1

Y	Japanese	Unit
yacht	ヨット（よっと）	9
years	とし	2
years old	さい	2
yellow	きいろ	12
yen (Japanese currency)	円（えん）	1
yes	はい；　ええ	1
yesterday	きのう	12
yoghurt	ヨーグルト（よーぐると）	10
you	あなた	6
younger brother	おとうと；おとうとさん	4
younger sister	いもうと；いもうとさん	4
your	あなたの	8
YouTube	ユーチューブ（ゆーちゅーぶ）	10

Z	Japanese	Unit
zero	ゼロ（ぜろ）；　れい	2

ISBN 9780170196826